A GUIDE
PHOTOGRAPHY
AND
THE SMOKY MOUNTAINS

A GUIDE TO
PHOTOGRAPHY
AND
THE SMOKY MOUNTAINS

PHOTOGRAPHS BY JOHN NETHERTON
TEXT BY DAVID DUHL AND JOHN NETHERTON

EDITED BY DAVID BADGER
CUMBERLAND VALLEY PRESS • NASHVILLE

ACKNOWLEDGEMENT

We would like to express our gratitude to the following who helped in some way to bring this book to fruition: Frank Carroll, Mark Carroll, Sara Carroll, David Badger, Donna Dangott, Don Defoe, Pete Garrett, Bob Godby, Gail Stephens, and Steve Kemp.

A special thanks to Fuji Photo Film USA Inc. for supplying the film for this project and to the naturalists and rangers of the National Park Service who have assisted us over the years.

Library of Congress Catalog Card Number: 88-70895
ISBN 0-9620582-0-3

Photographs © 1988 John Netherton
Text © 1988 John Netherton and David Duhl

Graphic Design/Layout: The Graf-iks Group, Inc., Nashville, TN
Typography: Comtype, Inc., Nashville, TN
Printed by Dai Nippon, Tokyo, Japan

FOREWORD

Ferns, Roaring Fork, 105mm lens, 1 second at f/16

As with all books, this cannot be all things to all people. We have tried to arrange it to fulfill two basic functions: to serve as a vehicle to help people develop photographic skills, and to provide means to appreciate the diversity of the Great Smoky Mountains National Park.

Parts I and II deal with photography. This approach is not intended to be en-cyclopedic, but, rather, one that should be used with the many fine instruction books and articles available today. The text is written for the 35mm camera user, and we hope it will appeal to all levels of photographer—amateur and professional.

Part III is about the park itself. We have provided the highlights, and we encourage you to use this book together with the guides the National Park Service offers on hiking trails, nature trails, streams and waterfalls, and much more. These guides, along with a series of nature identification books, are available at the park visitor centers; they, too, will enhance your appreciation of the Great Smoky Mountains National Park.

TABLE OF CONTENTS

INTRODUCTION

The Great Smoky Mountains National Park is 800 square miles of magnificent wilderness, yet it could rightfully be called America's backyard. With half the population of the United States living within a day's drive of its boundaries, it is no wonder that it hosts 10 million visitors annually. A drive anywhere in the park affords an inexhaustible variety of views of layered mountains stretching seemingly forever into the distance.

Yet these broad, sweeping vistas reveal only the canopy of the forest, nothing of the foundation from which it grows. Fifty yards off the roadside, one feels engulfed by primeval forest. The eye and mind ad- just to the restricted vision. Here is a beauty at once more intimate: variegated lichens, vibrant mosses, pastels of wildflowers. Patterns abound everywhere: the veination of a flower's petals, dappled sunlight on pine needles, fall leaves strewn on the moss-covered rocks along a rushing stream. Here, even the air is softer; one walks delicately.

The camera improves vision. The images produced are examined and re-examined. Not only does the knowledge of seeing in photographic terms increase, but so too do the appreciation and understanding of what is being photographed.

Variety and lushness are the hallmarks of the Smokies. The great range of elevations, from the valleys to the mountaintops, produces an astounding variety of habitats. Thus, through the seasons, some 1,500 species of flowering plants may be found, and more than 100 varieties of native trees—nearly as many as populate all of Europe. To capture on film something of the essence of the Smokies calls for a collection of images: the broad panorama of mountains to be sure, but also—and perhaps more importantly—the intimate view under the canopy of the Great Smoky Mountains.

Slimy salamander, Sugarlands, 55mm micro lens, 1 second at f/16

A CONSERVATION NOTE

The Great Smoky Mountains National Park is a treasure for all to enjoy. It is a plant and wildlife sanctuary, and all of us share a solemn obligation to preserve it. The picking of wildflowers, or any vegetation, for that matter, is strictly prohibited, as is harassing or feeding the wildlife. A complete listing of the rules and regulations of the park is available from the National Park Service or the ranger staff in the park.

The park rangers and naturalists are there to help you enjoy your visit. They will help you to interpret what you experience in the park and point you in the right direction to get the most out of your stay. They are knowledgeable and helpful; don't miss out on this resource.

It is the beauty and tonic of the outdoors that has lured us to this park. Please treat it with reverence, and remember the old saying: Take nothing but photographs, leave nothing but footprints.

Large-flowered trillium, Roaring Fork, 55mm micro lens, 2 seconds at f/22

EQUIPMENT

CAMERAS

One of the most frequently asked questions of photographers is: "What kind of camera do you have?" On one level, this is meant to be a flattering question, as in "I want to do that, too. What camera should I use?" Unfortunately, many people mean something altogether different, as in "You couldn't possibly have created something so beautiful. What camera did that?"

The fact is, once you get past the advertising propaganda of the camera companies, you soon realize that the truth lies somewhere in the middle: Cameras do exactly what the photographer wants.

This all assumes that the camera in question is of good quality, and almost all of the brand-name cameras satisfy this requirement. Other than brand loyalty, people choose one brand over another for two important reasons: optics and versatility.

When you buy a camera, you are really buying a system. While it is true that there are many fine independent lenses on the market, most people buy lenses made by the manufacturer of their camera. Since it's the optics (lenses) that are responsible for sharp pictures, people have traditionally gone with the brands with reputations for the highest quality optics. With computer-generated lenses and high quality control now commonplace, the differences between major brands are shrinking.

Most photographers need to be able to grow with their systems, so versatility becomes an important factor in choosing a camera system. It's the companies with the most varied lenses and accessories that attract photographers.

If you are looking to buy a new camera, go to your camera store, try out several there, see which one feels good in your hands and isn't awkward to use. Ask to see the company's catalog of lenses and talk to other photographers. This is an expensive investment; a sound choice will last you a lifetime. The fact remains, however, that any camera—from an Instamatic to a top-of-the-line 35mm—will bring you pleasure in the Smokies.

Frost on leaves, Clingmans Dome, 55mm micro lens, 6 seconds at f/22

Most people buy cameras with chrome bodies, but some prefer "professional" black bodies, which eliminate reflections and make the camera less visible. Whichever you prefer, one of the first choices you'll have to make is whether to acquire an automatic camera or a manual one.

While automatic cameras sound convenient, you must remember that a completely manual one is sufficient if you know how to use it properly. An automatic camera will do just fine in virtually all situations in the Smokies, but, again, you must know how to use it properly and when to manually override the metering system or compensate for the lighting.

For this reason, automatic cameras offer no real advantage. The new generation of auto-focus cameras offers no advantages, either; in fact, these introduce some real problems.

There are several features to consider when comparing cameras. The first is the depth-of-field preview button. This is one of the most useful features on a camera body, but, unfortunately, not all cameras have it.

Cameras meter with the lens wide open,

no matter what the aperture setting. By depressing the depth-of-field preview button, the camera will stop down to where you set it. The image in the viewfinder will get darker (less light gets through as the lens is stopped down), but what you are interested in is how much of the scene remains in focus. It's a good way to visualize the final image before you trip the shutter.

The second feature to consider is whether or not the camera will accept interchangeable focusing screens. Some have a split field in the center (which can be hard to use when photographing close-ups), others a matte surface, and some are completely clear. Still others have an etched grid to help keep horizons level, while some merely increase the overall brightness of the image (which has no effect on the amount of light hitting the film). Although it may be advantageous to have this flexibility, it is not essential.

Another decision you will have to make concerns the flash synchronization speed—that is, what is the fastest shutter speed you can use with an electronic flash? Faster shutter speeds mean less ghosting (that is, barely recognizable images caused by ambient light). If your flash can be used at 1/125 or 1/250 second, there won't be enough light to pick up this distraction.

Another factor to consider is the type of internal light meter used by the camera. Unfortunately, this varies from model to model even within the same brand line.

The two choices are the light emitting diode (LED) and the matched needle. Both have advantages and disadvantages. The LED is essentially a bright light that tells you when the exposure setting is correct, overexposed or underexposed. The advantage here is that you can see this no matter how little light illuminates your subject; the disadvantage is that after 1/2 stop, you really don't know how far off the correct exposure you are.

Conversely, the matched needles always let you know how far from the correct exposure you are set, but the needles are very hard to see in low light situations. Some cameras have a combination of the two: an LED that lights up next to a readout of camera settings. This has the advantages of both systems.

Many cameras have shutter mechanisms that are dependent on the camera battery for operation. If you are offered a choice, opt for a shutter that functions independently of batteries. Some of the newer cameras have one shutter speed that operates in such a manner—a useful feature when batteries lose their charge. Finally, many photographers object to the vibrations caused when the mirror moves from in front of the film as the shutter is tripped. In these situations, cameras capable of locking the mirror in the "up" position provide a satisfactory solution.

LENSES

The quality of the lenses you select may be the single most important technological factor contributing to a pleasing photograph. When you first enter the world of photography, you may not be able to discern a photograph taken with a superior lens from one taken with an inferior one. As you begin to grow and mature in this medium, the differences will become more apparent and justify the added expense of a fine lens.

Stream after heavy rains, Greenbrier, 28mm lens, 6 seconds at f/16

Spring foliage, Roaring Fork, 55mm micro lens, 1 second at f/22

Most photographers use only one system—the lenses and camera bodies manufactured by the same company. This ordinarily ensures consistency in quality and mechanics (all lenses manufactured by the same company will focus and will stop down in the same direction) not necessarily found by mixing lenses from independent manufacturers.

NORMAL LENSES

A normal lens (50mm) comes with most cameras; it has an angle of view similar to that of the human eye. Other lenses in the same focal-length range are more versatile, however. A 55mm macro lens, for example, will allow you to focus from 4 inches to infinity and still attain 1/2x magnification when used as a macro lens. Although a macro lens is slow compared to most normal lenses (f/3.5 vs. f/1.4 or f/1.8), this is seldom a drawback in the Smokies, where it will usually be used stopped down.

WIDE—ANGLE LENSES

Wide-angle lenses, although not often used for wildlife, can yield spectacular scenics. The three most frequently used wide-angle lenses are: the 20mm, for expansive sweeping vistas; the 24mm, for working in tight situations, such as in dense forest; and the 35mm lens, for areas a little more open, such as along streambanks.

If you have ever seen a photograph in which the trees appear to lean to the edge of the frame, you'll understand that distortion is a common problem when a wide-angle lens is first used. The distortion occurs when the lens is pointed at an upward or downward angle; the wider the lens, the more exaggerated the effect. To eliminate, or at least minimize, this distortion, position your camera at a level that does not require any tilting.

TELEPHOTO LENSES

Since they magnify objects at a distance, telephotos are the best type of lens to use when photographing wildlife or part of a stand of trees on a distant mountain.

Longer, however, does not always mean better, since the more you magnify your subject, the more you magnify movement. Achieving a sharp image of an active animal requires a fast shutter speed, and the typical telephoto lens with maximum aperture of f/5.6 or even f/4.5 will not always be fast enough. For this reason, if you plan to use a telephoto lens primarily for photographing wildlife, a fast lens (f/2.8 or f/4) is essential. But keep in mind that telephotos are big and expensive.

Stream in the fall, Greenbrier, 28mm lens, 4 seconds at f/16

Sunset and layering mountains, Clingmans Dome, 300mm lens, 1/4 second at f/8

It is advisable to use the shortest telephoto the situation will allow, usually in the range of 200-300mm. Also, since many telephoto lenses are not sharp at their maximum aperture, it may be necessary to stop yours down one stop from its widest aperture.

Finally, the new generation of telephoto lenses has two important characteristics worth noting. First, the glass is treated so that it has extra low dispersion (called ED glass), which means that all the colors in the spectrum should be in focus, even when shot wide open. Second, the new telephotos have internal focusing (IF) lenses. As a result, focusing actually takes place with the elements within the lens barrel, not by moving the front element toward or away from the film plane. This allows you to focus quickly—an advantage particularly notable with the longer telephoto lenses.

TELECONVERTERS

A teleconverter is a piece of optics which, when placed between the camera and lens, magnifies the image according to its designated power: 1.4x, 2x or 3x. For many years, teleconverters, like zoom lenses, were not considered very sharp, but that has now changed.

Although a 2x converter may sound powerful, it is not worth it, considering the light lost. For example, using it to convert a 200mm lens to 400mm will cause you to lose two f-stops, or to use a four-times longer shutter speed. A better alternative would be to use a 1.4x converter with a 300mm lens. This converts the lens to 420mm, but only costs you one f-stop.

ZOOM LENSES

For a long time, fixed focal length lenses were far superior to zoom lenses in sharpness. With improved technology, this generally is no longer true. In fact, zoom lenses have become standard equipment for most photographers.

Zoom lenses come in many ranges. Probably the most versatile is the 80-200mm, which is useful for scenics as well as for wildlife. Within this range, you can obtain full head shots of an animal by shooting at 200mm; then, by simply and effortlessly zooming out to 80mm, you can get full body shots of the same subject. Using fixed focal length lenses, you would have to change lenses (or change your position) each time you want to frame tighter or wider—and that's all it may take to frighten the animal away.

Zoom lenses, however, are heavier than most fixed focal length lenses and generally slower. They also have more elements, making them more susceptible to lens flare. A lens shade should always be used.

Sunrise and mountains, newfound Gap, 80-200 mm lens, 4 seconds at f/16

Mountainside in the fog, Morton Overlook, 80-200mm lens, 1 second at f/16

MACRO LENSES

A macro lens is useful when photographing small objects at high magnification, or when focusing close to a subject without losing light. The three most popular macro lenses have focal lengths of 55mm, 105mm and 200mm, and all are basically equal in quality. The lens of choice really depends upon what subjects you plan to photograph.

The 55mm macro is useful for photographing groundcovers, like mosses, or wildflowers with surrounding foliage. The 105mm and 200mm macro lenses are ideal for isolating subjects and for photographing subjects that won't allow a closer approach (e.g., butterflies, frogs and snakes). Of the three, the 200mm macro lens has the narrowest field of view; compared to the others, this lens incorporates less background within the photograph. This offers a great advantage when, for example, the horizon is behind a field of grass and you wish to eliminate it from the final image.

MIRROR LENSES

Mirror lenses have so many disadvantages that they are clearly the least desirable of all the telephoto lenses. They are generally slow, and they have a fixed aperture (usually f/8, although some are available at f/5.6). As a result of their optical design, out-of-focus highlights will appear as little doughnuts—usually very distracting. Although mirror lenses are less expensive and more compact, it's just not worth compromising your system for the longer focal length.

MACRO DEVICES

EXTENSION

The bellows is the most versatile close-up attachment made. It can be extended for

Green foliage with petals from crimson bee balm, Clingmans Dome, 105mm lens, 1 second at f/16

Passion flower, Cades Cove, 80-200mm lens with bellows, 1 second at f/22

more magnification by simply turning a knob, and, when used with an 80-200mm zoom lens, it can be focused from 4 to 40 inches without moving from one spot.

It is best to get an automatic bellows which requires no double cable release, and one with a double track that allows backward and forward movement of the whole system without changing magnification or position. Be extremely careful in the handling and storage of the bellows. Its fragile nature makes it prone to pinhole light leaks, which can cause fogging of the film. It's a good idea to collapse the bellows when not using it.

Keep in mind that, as you extend the bellows, there will be a corresponding loss of light for which you must compensate. The amount will vary depending on the extent of magnification. This can be easily calculated, or, more simply, the correct exposure can be determined by metering with the depth-of-field preview button depressed.

An extension tube is essentially a non-collapsing bellows. Like a bellows, it contains no glass and is designed to allow you to reduce the minimum focusing distance. These tubes come in various sizes (lengths) and fit between the camera and lens.

DIOPTER LENSES

For many years, these close-up attachments have had the reputation of being optically inferior. The major problem has always been the loss of sharpness around the edges as a result of the peripheral curvature of the lens. A number of manufacturers have resolved this and now produce high-quality diopter lenses.

The major advantage of this device is that no light is lost, as happens with many other close-up attachments. The diopter is also easy to use, since, like a filter, it screws onto the front element of the lens.

Leaf with drops of dew, Bud Ogle Nature Trail, 80-200mm lens with bellows, 1/2 second at f/8

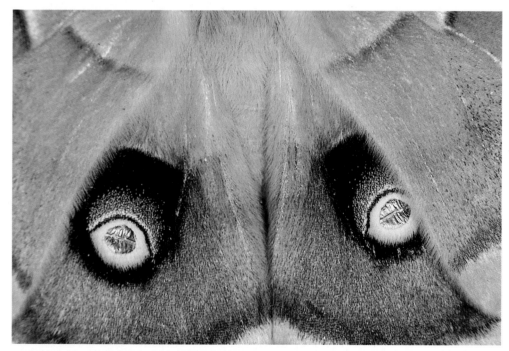

Polyphemus moth, Cades Cove, 80-200mm lens with bellows, 2 flash units, 1/60 second at f/22

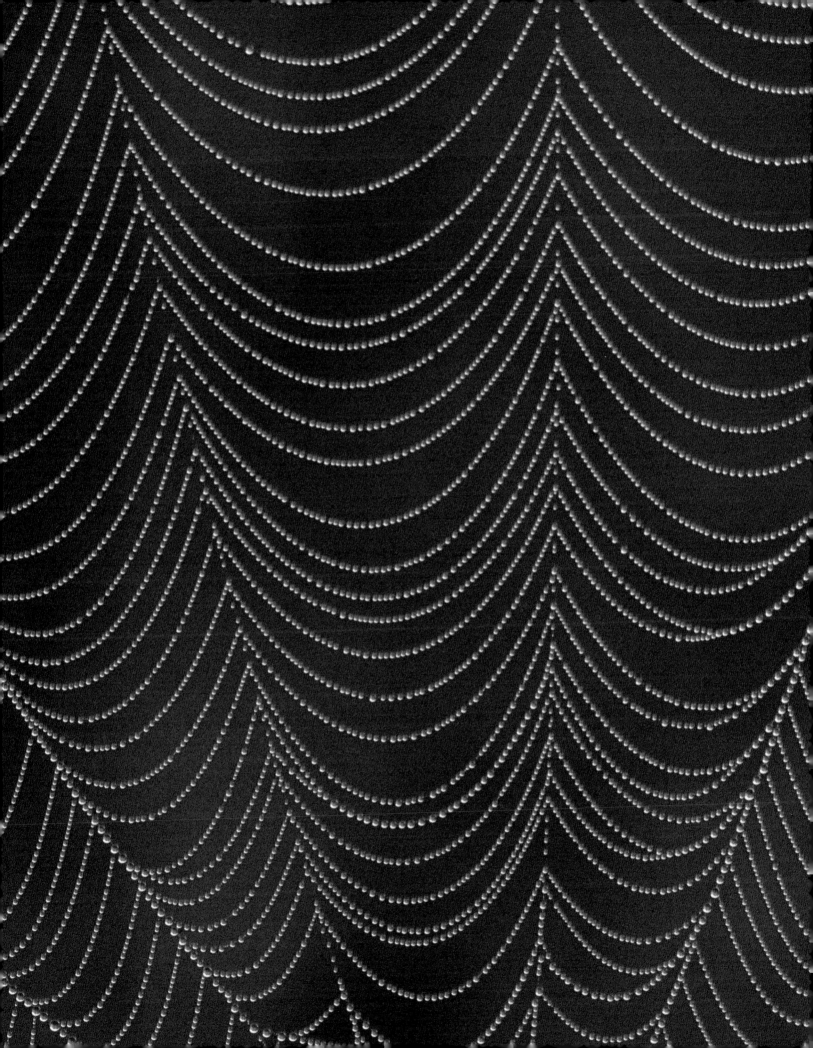

STACKING LENSES

A small, inexpensive lens-to-lens coupler will allow you to photograph with extreme magnification (3 to 5 times life-size). The primary lens ideally should be 100 to 200mm, and the stacked lens 35 to 80mm. The stacked lens is screwed onto the coupler in reverse, and focusing is accomplished by adjusting the camera-to-subject distance. Depth of field is very shallow, and you must be within several inches of your subject.

FILTERS

Filters are perhaps the most misused accessory a photographer owns. Like any other piece of equipment, filters should only be used with a specific photographic intent in mind. The better filters are made of high-quality optically corrected glass; they deserve the same care and attention as your best lens. In fact, some filter manufacturers make their own glass—the same they use for their top-of-the-line lenses.

If you've already spent the money for good optics, it makes sense to place a superior glass filter in front of the lens. This may cost a little more, but there is no reason to let your filters compromise the quality of your entire photographic system. If you are interested in saving money, buy a good filter and a step-up ring to adapt it to your smaller lenses, rather than an inferior-quality filter.

It is also advisable to avoid compromising the quality of your filters. Stacking of filters (i.e., using more than one at a time) should be kept to a minimum, since it can lead to lens flare and decreased contrast in the

Backlit leaf, Bud Ogle Nature Trail, 80-200mm lens with bellows, 1/4 second at f/8

Autumn colors reflecting in stream, Roaring Fork, 80-200mm lens, 1/15 second at f/8

final photograph. And, finally, remember that filters are designed to enhance the quality of your photograph, not to protect your lens.

POLARIZING FILTERS

This should be the most frequently used filter in the Smokies. Although polarizing filters can be used to darken blue skies and to reduce haze, their most common function is to deal with annoying reflections that occur on overcast and sunny days.

By rotating your polarizing filter, you can eliminate these reflections from streams, wet rocks and leaves, especially waxy leaves such as mountain laurel and rhododendron. Of course, some reflections are desirable, like fall colors reflecting in pools of water; these scenes need only partial polarization.

The best way to use a polarizing filter is to look through the viewfinder and rotate the filter until you see the desired effect. In general, a polarizing filter has its maximum impact when the lens is pointed 90 degrees with respect to the position of the sun.

Be extra careful if you use polarizing filters on extreme wide-angle lenses. First, large expanses of sky cannot always be darkened in their entirety, leaving only a section of the sky to appear dark blue. Secondly, vignetting can occur as the lens shade (or filter) is displaced from the front element of your lens. To check for this, simply point the camera at the bright sky, stop the lens down, press the depth-of-field preview button and examine the corners of the frame to see if the lens shade appears in the viewfinder.

Seasonal waterfall, roadside, 300mm lens, 6 seconds at f/22

WARMING FILTERS

The 81 series "warming" filters come in varying degrees: 81A, 81B and 81C (the 81C is the darkest in color). There is a common misconception that all overcast days tend to produce blue-biased images. While this is not always true, these filters are especially good at neutralizing the coolness that results when shooting in shade under a bright blue sky. Additionally, the stronger warming filters can be used to add color to a washed-out sunrise or sunset.

COLOR-COMPENSATING FILTERS

Color-compensating filters (known as CC filters) come in varying strengths; the "correct" filter is a matter of personal choice. The most commonly used CC filters are yellow, green, magenta, red and cyan. These filters are extremely delicate and usually come in square sheets that require a special attachment to hold them over the lens. Do not confuse these filters with acetate filters, which are neither optically corrected nor suitable for placement in front of your lens.

Gelatin filters have one significant drawback: They are adversely affected by the weather. Rain, fog and high humidity can cause gelatin filters to pucker and wrinkle, rendering them useless for all-weather photography. The alternative to the gelatin filter is a glass color-compensating filter, which lasts longer and is more versatile.

There are several situations in which color-compensating filters are particularly useful. In the shade, on a bright sunny day, colors tend to register on the film with a blue bias. By using a slight yellow-compensating filter, such as a CC 10Y, this can be corrected, although a warming filter in the 81 series could also correct this problem.

The greens in mountainscapes are usually quite vibrant without filtration, especially just after a rain. If you desire to intensify the color of the foliage further, use a slightly green CC filter, such as CC 10G or CC 5G.

Similarly, to intensify fall colors, a combination of CC 10Y and CC 5R is effective. Like

Fall leaf, Newfound Gap Road, 55mm micro lens, 3 seconds at f/16

Clinton's lily, Spruce-Fir Nature Trail, 105mm lens, 6 seconds at f/16

all filters, however, color-compensating filters should be used sparingly, and only when they contribute something to the final image.

NEUTRAL—DENSITY FILTERS

Neutral-density filters have no effect on the final color of a photograph; they simply decrease the amount of light hitting the

24

film and, therefore, require you to use longer exposures. In most cases in the Smokies—especially if you are using slow film—these filters are unnecessary. However, if you wish to use long exposures and the light is just too bright, a neutral-density filter may provide the solution.

These filters come in a variety of densities, resulting in a corresponding loss of speed. As a result, what was once several seconds in exposure can easily become one of several minutes with the right density filter. This may prove particularly useful when photographing a fast-flowing stream on a bright, sunny day. The effect will be water that appears silky, almost ethereal.

FILM

One important decision you will have to make before taking your first photograph is which film is right for you. Everyone has his or her own individual preferences and needs. If your intent is to showcase your photographs in a family album, then color print film is the film of choice.

But if you are looking for professional-quality results like the work you see reproduced in books and magazines, then a high-quality slide film must be used. Keep in mind, however, that slide film has less latitude than print film. That is, the proper exposure for slide film is critical, while print film offers more room for error.

Professional films are ready to be used at the time of sale, while amateur films—which are expected to maintain a longer shelf life—actually mature on the shelf. For this reason, professional films are more consistent in color and balance. They should always be refrigerated until use, and it's wise to allow an hour for the film to warm up before removing it from the canister. As repeated warming and cooling can affect color, it's best to hold this to a minimum.

Many photographers tend to use the newest high-speed films available. These films, however, are usually quite grainy and have poor color rendition compared with slower films. Such films will not be discussed here.

Fall foliage in fog, Newfound Gap Road, 80-200mm lens, 3 seconds at f/16

Mountains in fog after sunset, Morton Overlook, 80-200mm lens, 15 seconds at f/11

COLOR FILMS

Fujichrome 50 Professional. This film has recently become very popular with photographers and publishers. While it's true that the colors are not always realistic, they are nonetheless quite pleasing. The reds are almost as brilliant as with Kodachrome 25, while the greens and blues are so vibrant that no other film even comes close. The resolution is as fine as Kodachrome 64, and Fujichrome is E-6 compatible, allowing for same-day processing. When shooting in the shade or on a sunny day, some color correction will be required to prevent the subject from exhibiting more blue tones than normal.

Kodachrome 25 Professional. Kodachrome 25 has the finest resolution of any color film on the market today. The reds and yellows are vibrant, and the greens are true to color. Kodachromes are more stable than E-6 films and are said to last up to 100 years (Ektachrome and Fujichrome last for 50 years).

Kodachrome 64 Professional. Kodachrome 64 is not as fine-grained as Kodachrome 25. It is higher in contrast, and it offers 1 1/3 stops more speed than Kodachrome 25 and about 1/3 stop more than Fujichrome 50. Many wildlife photographers find this extra speed to be a great advantage. Kodachrome 64 has a tendency, however, to shift to the magenta on long exposures. This shows up quite clearly on snow, or on other subjects with white or neutral colors.

Ektachrome 100. Ektachrome 100 is more neutral in color than the old Ektachrome, which used to exhibit a bluish cast. It can be processed locally at any custom E-6 lab, which allows for same-day service.

Color Print Film. Most nature photographers do not use color print films (e.g.,

Kodacolor 100, 200 or 400), but these films can yield satisfactory results if properly handled. Again, the slower the film, the less grain you will have. Exposures differ from slide film, however. With slide film, slight underexposure (1/3 to 1/2 stop) sometimes results in greater color saturation, while with print film, underexposure can result in muddy-looking prints with no detail in the shadows. If in doubt, overexpose slightly with color print film.

CARE and HANDLING

Extreme heat affects color and should always be avoided. Glove compartments and car trunks especially should never be used for film (or film-loaded camera) storage during warm weather. On the other hand, cold weather poses special problems, too. Film becomes brittle when exposed to subfreezing conditions, so it should be advanced slowly to avoid static marks or breakage.

PROCESSING

Quality processing is just as important as using good film. Discount processors abound, but films suffer for it. Most major cities have E-6 custom-processing labs, and mailers for the major film companies are available throughout the United States. If in doubt, contact a professional photographer in your town and inquire where his or her film is processed. Note, too, that film should always be processed promptly.

TRIPODS

One of the most important pieces of equipment required to shoot consistently good photographs is a tripod. Yet, oddly enough, this device is habitually overlooked as an essential piece of photographic equipment.

Most people think to use a tripod for long exposures, but the truth of the matter is that a tripod is useful for *all* exposure times. Not only does it steady the camera, but it also allows you to compose your picture more effectively. Since the camera is stationary, you can carefully check the edges and corners in the viewfinder without the slight changes that hand-holding your camera creates.

The tripod should steady your camera and eliminate vibrations. Since vibrations are primarily caused by touching the camera or by the wind, a tripod makes it easier to avoid these problems. Always use a cable release (or, for short exposures, the self-timer) and use a tripod that you know is sturdy.

Some of the lighter-weight tripods are handy for backpacking or for mounting remote flash or mirrors, but you really should use the best one available for your camera. If it is a particularly windy day, you can even add weight (a bag filled with rocks, for example) to the center post of the tripod to help sturdy it.

Many photographers buy tripods that are too short. A good tripod will reach to at least eye level with the legs (but not the center column) extended. Since you get maximum stability by keeping the center of gravity as low as possible, the height of the tripod should be changed by adjusting the legs, not the center column. Tripod legs should be capable of quick extension, with a minimum of effort; for maximum versatility in the field, the legs should be capable of shifting 90 degrees to horizontal.

A number of good heads are available that fit all tripods. Once again, the key is versatility. Many people use tripod heads with separate locks for horizontal and vertical positions. These are very sturdy and

Fall leaves, Newfound Gap Road, 80-200mm lens, 6 seconds at f/16

allow you to pan in one direction while holding fast in the other. Yet many photographers also find them awkward to use and prefer ball-and-socket heads. When loosened, these heads allow for complete freedom of movement, and a slight fastening of a set screw holds the camera in position. Ball-and-socket heads are fast and easy to use, but you must select one that is sturdy enough to support your heaviest camera and lens combination.

Eastern box turtle, Oconaluftee, 80-200mm lens with bellows, 2 flash units, 1/60 second at f/11

FLASH

In the Smoky Mountains, flash is best used when photographing wildlife. For close-ups of insects, amphibians and reptiles, it can effectively stop movement. For large mammals, like deer and bears, it can be used to fill in the already existing light or to add a highlight to the eyes. Whatever the use, several factors should be considered when choosing a flash.

Guide numbers, calculated with ASA 50 film, should range between 35 and 125, depending on whether you plan to do more close-up or large mammal photography (for outdoor flash using manual settings, it is important to calibrate the power of your flash by bracketing). You will need a less powerful flash for close-up

work, and, obviously, more power when shooting animals at longer distances. The best choice is a flash with variable power levels, which will permit both.

Light from some of the more powerful flashes can be surprisingly harsh. Some units are sold with diffusers, but a piece of acetate can also be taped over a flash to achieve the same effect. Though less of a problem with the newer flashes, light can sometimes be cold-looking. Again, this problem can be solved by taping a warming filter over the flash or by inserting a filter between the diffuser and the flash.

Recycling time on a flash can be important if you need to shoot frames in quick succession. Many flash units can be plugged into a lightweight rechargeable battery pack to provide fast recycling

and more flashes than conventional batteries. The pack can be strapped onto a belt or worn on the shoulder with a camera strap.

MULTIPLE FLASH

When engaging in close-up photography of subjects like butterflies, frogs, salamanders or snakes, it is best to use two flash units—one mounted on each side of the camera—to avoid shadows. Both units can be shot at the same power, or, for additional modeling, one can be reduced to 1/2 or 1/4 power. If you anticipate using two flashes in this way, both units should be exactly alike (otherwise the calculating of exposure can be enormously frustrating).

If your subject is stationary, or if you know it will return to a certain location (for example, a flower), then one flash can be mounted on a tripod and positioned to sidelight or backlight the subject, while the second flash is mounted to a bracket connected to the camera. By attaching a photosensitive device (or ''slave unit'') to the flash on the tripod, both will go off when the picture is taken.

FILL FLASH

When photographing birds and mammals, natural light may be overcast and lifeless, or sunny and high-contrast with harsh shadows. In either case, fill flash can rectify these problems. On an overcast day, your subject may only require a catchlight in the eye or need to be 1/3 stop brighter than its background. This is the time to use fill flash on automatic setting, according to how much light you require to illuminate your subject.

For example, on an overcast day, the proper exposure is 1/60 second at f/5.6. To use fill flash, shoot at this same shutter speed and aperture combination, and set the flash on the automatic mode of f/2.8, two stops under the true reading. This will provide just enough light to make the subject stand out.

On sunny days, when the sun provides backlighting or your subject turns its head into a shadow, use the same approach for fill flash, but this time set the flash only one stop off your meter reading for sufficient light. It is important that fill flash not be the dominant light source in daylight photographs of animals, or it will not look natural.

While automatic flashes are rarely reliable for close-up photography (they assume the lens is directly attached to the camera, and so do not take into account any loss of light from extension with a bellows or tube), they work well for fill flash as long as the background is not overly dark.

If necessary, the flash can be removed from the camera by using brackets with small ball heads to adjust the angle of the flash. Don't try to hand-hold the flash—you'll be unable to focus or advance your film after the first exposure.

FLASH METERS

If you are unsure of the proper exposure

Gray tree frog silhouette, Sugarlands, 55mm micro lens, 1 flash, 1/60 second at f/22

with a flash, or if you are setting up a complex multiple-lighting shot, you may find a flash meter useful for measuring the intensity of the light. As a bonus, some units also serve as ambient light meters.

Tree in fog, Newfound Gap Road, 300mm lens, 1 second at f/16

EXPOSURE

Camera meters are calibrated against middle gray. That is, they are programmed to relate the light intensity to the amount theoretically reflecting off a gray surface (specifically, a gray surface that reflects 18% of the light hitting it). Thus, the camera meter does not distinguish between white or black objects. To the camera meter, a white object is a gray one with much light reflecting off it, while a black object is a gray one with little light reflecting. Because your camera meter is calibrated for gray, these objects would result in under- and overexposure, respectively.

Success in proper metering lies in recognizing when a subject is not reflecting light like an 18% gray subject and then compensating for it. All things considered, the best solution is to find something in the scene that is middle-toned, meter off it, recompose and shoot at the setting for the middle-gray subject.

Some photographers prefer to carry an 18% gray card with them, but this is not necessary if you meter a subject such as your camera bag and note how far from middle-gray it is.

Another problem is that most camera meters do not give the correct reading. However, by calibrating your camera meter, or by determining how far from middle gray your camera meter is under various conditions, you can obtain accurate meter readings. Most camera meters are calibrated for print film, and so are biased toward overexposure. For this reason, an exposure 1/3 to 1/2 under that indicated by an uncalibrated light meter will yield more saturated colors on slide film.

You can calibrate your camera's light meter simply by metering on a gray card and comparing the settings you get (for correct exposure) to ones taken with a calibrated meter—for example, another camera that has already been calibrated. If the settings differ, then adjust the ASA until both cameras meter identically. Essentially, this will accomplish what the manufacturers should have done at the factory—set up the camera to provide a reliable middle-gray reading.

As an alternative, you can take advantage of the fact that, on a sunny day, the correct camera setting can be calculated with the formula 1/film speed (1/60 second for ASA 64 film, for example) at f/16. This "sunny 16" rule can come in handy when your light meter fails or when you need to calibrate your camera.

Simply set your camera at 1/film speed at f/16 and meter on a gray card on a bright sunny day. If your light meter does not read this as a correct exposure, change the ASA setting until it does.

In the Smokies, situations which commonly require compensation occur when shooting in snow or fog. In both instances, subjects tend to be underexposed because the light meter is "fooled" by the brightness from the white snow or the luminous fog.

The solution in both cases is the same. Find a nearby object that is middle gray and fills the frame; take a meter reading; then recompose the photograph and shoot without remetering.

Alternatively, since you know the subject will be underexposed, take an initial meter reading and overexpose. Just how much to overexpose will be based on personal experience, but, in general, about 1/2 stop for fog and one to two stops for snow. Of course, a great deal also depends on the overall brightness of the scene, frontlighting versus backlighting, and the mood you wish to create.

No matter how you meter, one special situation merits attention: film reciprocity failure. With most films, photographs become underexposed with exposures greater than one second, creating a problem when photographing for great depth of field in dimly lit areas. This is simply a failure of the film to respond to light at long exposures in the same way it does at short ones.

For both Kodachrome and Fujichrome films, an exposure from 2 seconds to about 30 seconds needs an additional 50% exposure. If, for example, your light meter indicates a 4-second exposure at f/16, adding 50% makes the corrected exposure 4 seconds between f/16 and f/11, or 6 seconds at f/16 if you do not want to sacrifice depth of field.

Anything from 30 seconds to three minutes simply requires doubling the exposure time; after three minutes, it's too hard to predict, so you may want to bracket. Some film manufacturers don't recommend long exposures like this and claim there is an accompanying color shift. But, for almost all work in the field, there doesn't seem to be any noticeable effect.

When photographing in situations where you cannot get a meter reading—for example, 30 minutes before sunrise—open the lens to its widest aperture and set the shutter speed to the slowest that will register a meter reading. This will indicate the camera setting to use to provide a correctly exposed photograph (and, remember, you can use this or any equivalent shutter-aperture combination).

If you still cannot obtain a meter reading under this low-light condition, start changing the ASA setting—in effect, telling the camera to regard the film as more sensitive to light than it actually is. But keep in mind that this is purely a mathematical exercise; you are not changing the sensitivity of the film from what the manufacturer produced.

For example, if your film is rated at 50 and you don't get a reading to set the ASA at 100, then just double the exposure indicated. If you don't register a reading until ASA 200, then increase your exposure 4x (doubling the exposure twice). When you are finished, remember to return your camera to the ASA setting compatible with your film.

LIGHT

Lighting—i.e., the quality and direction of light—is one of the least-considered aspects of photography, yet it easily sets great photographs apart from average ones. Compared to the cold, harsh light of the midday sun, early-morning and late-afternoon light projects a warmth that is very flattering to most photographic subjects. For this reason, many photographers shoot only at these two times of day.

Similarly, most nature photographers prefer photographing under the even lighting conditions of an overcast day. This conveniently avoids harsh shadows and hot spots that are distracting and that the film often cannot record with detail.

BACKLIGHTING

In many instances, the quality of light attracts attention to a particular scene. Of all the possible lighting situations, backlighting can produce some of the finest, if most troublesome, photographs. Trees or leaves that are backlit create a feeling of depth, as they seem to be separated from a nonbacklit background.

Because you are shooting into the bright sun, your camera meter will give a false reading, resulting in an underexposed photograph. The solution is simple: Approach the subject and meter directly off it (keeping it backlit), or take your initial meter reading and overexpose one to two stops. In a situation like this, where there is no single correct exposure, it really depends on the mood you wish to create.

There are many situations in which backlighting can isolate an animal from its background—often an advantage, since numerous species are marked or colored to blend in with their environment. In addition, the veination of leaves is clearly defined when sunlight shines through, yielding a much more interesting photograph. Silhouettes of insects and spiders, or frogs perched on a leaf, can prove far more striking than the same subjects frontlit.

MIRRORS

Sometimes lighting requires enhancement. When flash is too harsh, or when cloth reflectors fail to direct the light, mir-

Chrysalis backlit by sun, Cades Cove, 80-200mm lens with bellows, 1/4 second at f/5.6

Chrysalis backlit by sun and illuminated frontally by mirrors, 1/4 second at f/11

rors may provide the solution. Mirrors can be used to backlight, sidelight or frontlight a subject, or they can fill in a shadow area by reflecting light where directed. Mirrors are useful not just on sunny days; on overcast days they may also provide enough light to fill in the dark underside of a flower, or prompt a caterpillar to stand out from its background.

While any mirror will serve this purpose, unbreakable plastic or metal mirrors are more practical for fieldwork. You won't need anything larger than 5 x 7 inches, and by mounting the mirror to a wooden frame and threading the bottom to fit your tripod, you will be able to direct light while leaving your hands free.

NOCTURNAL PHOTOGRAPHY

Illuminating a subject to provide sharp focus and composition is the greatest obstacle encountered in nocturnal photography. To compound the difficulty, some animals will turn their heads or fly away when white light is used.

Since most nocturnal creatures are extremely sensitive to low light but generally have poor color vision, they can be illuminated by red light with little, if any, impact on behavior. In addition, red light provides enough illumination to move about and check your gear and camera settings without losing your bearings in the dark.

Red acetate, purchased from a theatrical supply house, is useful for covering a light source such as a flashlight or miner's headlight. A car hose clamp can be used to connect the light source to your flash unit. In this way, you can point your camera any direction and have a beam of light properly aligned with your subject. Only minor adjustments need to be made as the subject-to-camera distance changes. If focusing with a red light proves difficult, you can replace your split-focusing screen with a brighter one or try a faster lens.

To photograph animals at night, you will need to illuminate your subjects with flash units. Two flash heads are recommended to eliminate the harsh shadow cast by just one. Some flash units have built-in brackets to permit attachment of more than one at a time. If your units do not have brackets, consider making or purchasing a simple adapter to provide this option.

Flash units set on automatic work quite well (provided you've checked them first). In addition, since two units likely will not discharge completely on automatic, the recycling time will be reduced.

If you prefer to use units in the manual mode, remember that most flashes are calibrated for indoor use; consequently, when shooting outside at night, the correct exposure will differ from that recommended by the manufacturer. This is approximately a 2 f-stop difference, depending on the distance from flash to

Spider silhouetted against setting sun, near Oconaluftee, 80-200mm lens with bellows, 1/60 second at f/4.5

Opossum with young, Smokemont, 80-200mm lens, 2 flash units, 1/60 second at f/8

subject, and it must be calibrated for your own system.

First, make several trial shots outdoors with your flash in the manual mode. Then evaluate how underexposed the resulting photograph is and make a note to compensate by changing the power ratios, subject-to-flash distance or ASA setting of the flash.

WEATHER

Photography under adverse weather conditions often results in uniquely successful photographs. Whether you're shooting in snow, rain or fog, you are likelier to produce something of interest than with the same subject on a clear, bright day. In the Smokies, you may be able to take some of your best photographs when tourists are beating a hasty retreat down the mountains because of inclement conditions.

FOG

Because of its mystical qualities, fog can provide some glorious opportunities for a photographer. In fog, landscape images can become ethereal and almost impressionistic. Mountains appear separated, as if shrouded in secrecy, while colors become muted into soft pastels. Photographing in fog need not be difficult, but a few pointers should be heeded.

The water droplets in fog have tremendous luminance. Since a light meter is calibrated for middle gray, a faulty meter reading will result unless you compensate for it (see section on exposure). Opening up 1/2 stop more than your light meter indicates will usually suffice when photographing in or into fog. On rare occasions, however, the fog may be so thick (and bright) that a correction of up to 3/4 stop is required.

Keep in mind that an underexposed fog image is dull and lifeless, while one properly exposed is vibrant and crisp. If you are unsure which setting to use, bracket your exposures and start at 1/2 stop over what your light meter indicates.

If you need to use a warming filter, be aware that gelatin-type filters respond to moisture in the fog by buckling and distorting their shape. Experiment with dif-

Fog and mountains, near Newfound Gap, 80-200mm lens, 1 second at f/11

Trees in mist, near Chimneys Picnic Area, 80-200mm lens, 6 seconds at f/16

ferent color-correction filters, then select those glass filters that you prefer.

One of the best times to photograph in the fog is early morning. Many photographers drive up to higher elevations at this hour expressly in search of fog.

In spite of appearances, the fog is constantly moving. When the Sugarlands Visitor Center is under blue skies, the Clingmans Dome and Newfound Gap areas can be completely fogged in. Fortunately, this may work to your advantage, since most visitors prefer blue skies and tend to avoid the fog. As a result, they also shun the view from Clingmans Dome of the mountain peaks and fog-laden valleys below.

Late evening, when most visitors are winding their way back down the mountain, is another fine time to photograph in the fog. One particularly good site is Morton Overlook, which faces west. Just around sunset, the fog comes drifting in here. While traffic passes you by, you will be making 30-second to one-minute exposures of fog in one of the most scenic pulloffs in the park.

Although your vision will at times be severely limited by the fog, your creativity will not. Altogether different moods can be captured when the same subject is photographed with and without fog. Furthermore, quite ordinary scenes with no inherent interest can be made more inviting when photographed in fog. Creative photographers, aware that fog will soon converge on an area, will wait patiently for such a scene to come alive.

Anticipation can make all the difference between an ordinary photograph and a beautiful image. Because the fog changes constantly, your film can capture more of a foggy scene than you might at

Light snow on trees, Newfound Gap Road, 80-200mm lens, 1 second at f/22

first imagine. Some expanses will be quite clear, some shrouded in fog, some barely detectable. To capture such a potentially mystical image, shoot with maximum depth of field, stopping down to f/22 or f/32.

RAIN

When it rains in the Smokies, visitors generally begin the caravan down the mountain. Yet this is one of the best times to photograph.

During—or just after—a rain, colors appear more vibrant and saturated. Lichens that blended into the drab tree trunks are now dark green and contrast the dark trunks. Mosses on boulders stand out against their wet backgrounds. Fall colors take on a new glow. The accompanying overcast light allows detail to be recorded on the undersides of boulders and under

the canopies of trees—details usually lost on sunny days.

The greatest problem photographing under these conditions is keeping the rain off the front element of your lens—especially a wide-angle lens—and out of your photographic equipment. Always use a lens hood, and if you work with a tripod, hold an umbrella over the camera. Or, better yet, attach the umbrella directly to the tripod, leaving your hands free. Once you've composed and metered, remove the umbrella so it won't be a source of vibration when you take the photograph.

When not actually shooting, use a plastic trash bag to cover the camera and lens. It's also a good idea to keep a towel handy to wipe the moisture from your equipment.

WINTER

Winter temperatures may be comfortable around Cades Cove and Sugarlands, while well below freezing at the higher elevations of Newfound Gap and Clingmans Dome. Snows of 8 to 12 inches are not uncommon, but rarely last more than two or three days before melting. It is important, therefore, to be present during, or shortly after, the snowfalls in order to get good photographs.

Freshly fallen snow on bare trees or on needles of evergreens seems to be a popular wintertime subject, but don't overlook the elegant patterns created by melting ice or the juxtaposition of melting and frozen snow. Snow is most frequent in January or February, but heaviest in March.

During the winter, the Cades Cove Loop Road opens at sunrise unless roads are covered with snow or ice. Roaring Fork and Clingmans Dome are closed from Dec. 1 until March or April. The park has two telephone numbers to call for weather conditions: (615) 436-5615 for the Tennessee side and (704) 497-9146 for North Carolina.

Several important considerations in winter photography should be noted. First, after you have been out in the cold with equipment, do not take your camera or lenses out of the case in a warm room. Condensation will form on the glass surfaces unless you leave all your gear in the case and let it warm up gradually.

Next, if your lens has dust on it, do not try to blow it off; your breath will create a layer of frost on the front element. Instead, use a blower brush sold in photo stores.

Your tripod and metal camera bodies can also get very cold. Try not to touch them with your bare hands. And when conditions get messy, be careful to keep water or melting snow off your equipment.

Snow also requires special considerations in metering. Since there are no middle tones in white snow, an overexposure of 3/4 to 1 1/2 f-stops is required. This decision will depend on the mood you wish to convey: The more you overexpose, the less detail will emerge in the snow and the colder it will appear to be.

On a sunny day, under a brilliant blue sky, the shadow areas in snow appear extremely blue. If your subject is entirely in the shade, a warming filter can be used to correct the blue cast. If you use this approach when photographing a combination of shadows and sunlight, the sunlit areas will take on the coloration of your warming filter.

Snow-covered trees, near Newfound Gap, 80-200mm lens, ¼ second at f/16

Sunrise with layered mountains, Newfound Gap, 80-200mm lens, 6 seconds at f/16

MOUNTAIN-SCAPES

One of the first images people summon to mind when thinking of the Smoky Mountains is the layering of mountain upon mountain on the horizon. Most visitors photograph this scene with a normal or wide-angle lens. Unfortunately, this generally reduces the mountains to mere specks in the distance, with distracting sky and foreground. It's much more effective to use a medium telephoto lens to isolate particular areas; the resulting compression will restore the original vision.

Metering for mountainscapes is really quite simple. Consider the case of New-found Gap at daybreak. The near ridge, running diagonally through the viewfinder, will be in silhouette, while the mountains in the background will probably be in haze. These hazy mountains are the area on which to meter, stopping down 1/2 to 1 full f-stop. As long as the sky is not overly bright, it will retain its brilliant color. It is still important to use a small aperture, even though the far mountains are obscured, for their outlines need to be focused sharply.

Mountains conjure up an image of large stationary objects, and this will work to your advantage if you use them as a backdrop for some other mountainscape scene. For example, if you position the ridges—which usually run diagonally—across the image, you will transform them into subjects full of visual motion.

Similarly, if you photograph treelines or patterns of bare trunks on a mountainside, you will be demonstrating the paradox of delicate patterns at rest on their bulky hosts—a highly satisfying approach to photographing mountains.

STREAMS, WATERFALLS and POOLS

A silky-looking stream or cascading waterfall adds serenity to an image. But to achieve this, a slow shutter speed is required. An exposure time of 1/2 second or longer is sufficient to blend the spraying water into a continuous body. This effect will only occur, however, when the water is spraying over rocks or cascading over ledges. If the water flows fast over a multitude of rocks in a stream, a long exposure, ranging into the minutes, will transform the silky look into a low-flowing fog.

If you prefer to convey the power of the flowing water, a faster shutter speed—on the order of 1/250 second—will be required. By way of comparison, the human eye perceives water movement at 1/30 to 1/60 second; you may wish to shoot a "literal" photograph at this shutter speed.

A polarizing filter is particularly effective when photographing streams and waterfalls, since wet rocks are highly reflective. A polarizing filter will not only remove the annoying highlights, but it will also bring out the browns of the rocks and greens of the mosses.

Not all streams and waterfalls should be photographed from a close position. Trees and foliage, for example, can frame a stream quite eloquently. The human eye, after all, usually views streams from a road or path.

If you are using a wide-angle lens to frame a stream or waterfall, or a telephoto lens to isolate a certain area, beware of spraying water. Droplets on the front element of a filter or lens will register as distortions on the final image. Furthermore, rocks near

Mountain brook, Roaring Fork, 80-200mm lens, 6 seconds at f/22

Water spraying at bottom of falls, Grotto Falls, 80-200mm lens, 6 seconds at f/16

Falls after a heavy rain, Grotto Falls, 28mm lens, 6 seconds at f/16

water can be slippery; take extra care to be sure your tripod is secure.

Water scenes in the park are best photographed on overcast days. This is because the even lighting results in a more pleasing final image. The film simply cannot handle the contrast of the highly reflective water and the dark boulders in the shadow areas.

ABRAMS FALLS

Abrams Falls is one of the more spectacular waterfalls in the park. Cascading over a rock ledge, the water falls approximately 20 feet into a large pool, finally draining into Abrams Creek. Unfortunately, a large tree has toppled here, and it lies diagonally across a portion of the falls. By positioning yourself on the rocks just downstream of the falls, you can attain a good vantage point. With a 24mm lens, the falls can be seen in the upper left-hand portion of the frame, while the creek and white foaming water lead the eye across the picture.

GROTTO FALLS

Grotto Falls plunges over a ledge to a small pool below. The area around the falls is more open than some and allows for a wide variety of angles. There are, however, several large boulders some 50 feet in front of the falls, requiring a closer working distance. By including these boulders, a sense of depth and strength is added to the image. A vertical format works well here, especially with a wide-angle 35mm or 28mm lens. Including the green foliage above the falls adds color to the final image.

One unique feature of Grotto Falls is that the trail actually passes behind the falls, suggesting additional photographic opportunities. Shooting the falls from the back side creates a dynamic perspective not often seen.

HEN WALLOW FALLS

This falls is difficult to frame—especially horizontally—because of its unusual dimensions: Only 3 feet wide at the top, it widens to 15 feet at the bottom. The water cascades and runs down the rock face, sometimes separating into three individual falls. The best approach is to isolate areas with a telephoto lens.

INDIAN CREEK FALLS

Rather than dropping straight over a ledge, Indian Creek Falls runs diagonally from the observer's point of view, falling 40 feet over the rocks. The best angle is just to the right of the falls, using a wide-angle lens to include the moss-covered boulders and surrounding foliage. A horizontal format that includes the pool of water at the bottom left works well here.

JUNEYWHANK FALLS

Juneywhank is one of the less spectacular falls in the park; were it not for the incline, it would be considered a small stream. During the spring and summer, foliage surrounds the falls, and after a good rain some effective tightly cropped pictures can be shot.

LAUREL FALLS

The trail to Laurel Falls is one of the smoothest and shortest in the park. The trail, which leads to the top of the falls, is very popular, so if you don't want hikers in your photograph, you'll have to get there early.

There are a number of large boulders and fallen trees close to the bottom of the falls, allowing you to set up your tripod without getting your feet wet. From this vantage point, you'll be able to frame the falls with the surrounding mountain laurel foliage.

Reflections in a stream, Deep Creek, 300mm lens, 1/15 second at f/5.6

MEIGS FALLS

Meigs Falls is especially photogenic after heavy summer showers or autumn rain. Most people shoot from the roadside (approximately 100 yards from the falls), since the alternative is to wade the Little River. Yet it is definitely worth crossing the river if you can negotiate the slippery rocks. In the summer months, brilliant green mosses, wet from the spray, cling to the rock wall. In the foreground, note the small creek that eventually drains into the Little River.

Falls on an overcast day, Meigs Falls, 28mm lens, 12 seconds at f/16

Isolated section of falls, Mingo Falls, 300mm lens, 6 seconds at f/16

MINGO FALLS

Mingo Falls cascades approximately 120 feet down a rock wall. Because of the steep drop, considerable rainfall is needed to produce more than a trickle of water over the rocks. As winter snows melt, water becomes more plentiful, causing spray to fly across the whole face of the rock ledge.

To shoot the entire falls, a wide-angle lens is required, pointed at an upward angle. Alternatively, a 200mm lens can be used to isolate the ledges and cascades, with the water taking on a look of silk at slow shutter speeds.

RAINBOW FALLS

Rainbow Falls is located on one of the trails that leads to the top of Mount Le Conte. This is one of the longer trails, so be prepared to spend a good part of the day here.

The falls spray water more than 80 feet over rock ledges, and light from the afternoon sun forms a rainbow in the spray. The entire falls need not be in the photograph. Isolating the section of the falls with the rainbow and using a long exposure to capture the silky look of the water can be quite effective.

RAMSAY CASCADES

This is one of the highest falls in the park. During heavy rains, the water crashes against an outcropping of the ledge. Shoot these falls with a fast shutter speed to illustrate the force and sculpting power of the water. A wide-angle lens can be used from the area by the footbridge, or try a telephoto lens to isolate water spraying over the ledge.

SINKS

The Sinks is really a small river running over a series of large boulders, finally plunging 15 feet where the river bends.

The water appears black at the base of the rock located to the left of the parking area.

There are a number of vantage points from which to photograph—mostly straight on or pointing downward. No mosses or lichens grow on the boulders, however, so unless you include some of the surrounding trees, the photograph will look monochromatic.

THE PLACE OF A THOUSAND DRIPS
This cascade, located just by the roadside, is appropriately named. The water sprays over several ledges into hundreds of little streams. Some areas are covered with mosses and liverworts, nourished by a steady trickle of water. A telephoto lens will enable you to frame shots that could otherwise only be achieved by climbing the slippery mountainside.

TOMS BRANCH FALLS
Toms Branch Falls is just off an old roadbed across the stream in Deep Creek. It is so overgrown with trees that the foliage obscures most of the view of the falls. During spring and fall, when the foliage is less dense, a medium telephoto lens will allow you to isolate several areas, especially those that empty into the stream.

POOLS
Fast-flowing streams may be interrupted by, or pass alongside, pockets of water that otherwise appear to stand motionless. This is where leaves collect. In autumn, the reds of maples, yellows of poplars and browns of fallen pine needles seem suspended in space as they create a mosaic of color. Sometimes the effect is disorienting, however, and it may be necessary to include a rock in the water to add stability to the photograph.

A polarizing filter is frequently necessary to eliminate the reflections from the water's surface and the submerged leaves. Note, however, that the yellows and reds in the trees above, and the blues of the sky, may reflect magnificent colors in the water that the polarizer will eliminate.

Rocks in autumn pool, Deep Creek, 80-200mm lens, 1 second at f/11

WATERFALL LOCATION GUIDE

WATERFALL	GENERAL LOCATION	ROUND TRIP
Abrams Falls	Cades Cove	5 miles
Grotto Falls	Roaring Fork	3 miles
Hen Wallow Falls	Cosby	4 miles
Indian Creek Falls	Deep Creek	2 miles
Juneywhank Falls	Deep Creek	1.5 miles
Laurel Falls	Little River Road	2.5 miles
Meigs Falls	Little River Road	Roadside
Mingo Falls	Big Cove Road	0.5 miles
Place of 1,000 Drips	Roaring Fork	Roadside
Rainbow Falls	Roaring Fork	5.5 miles
Ramsay Cascades	Greenbrier	8 miles
The Sinks	Little River Road	Roadside
Toms Branch Falls	Deep Creek	0.5 miles

Bottom of Mingo Falls, 80-200mm lens, 3 seconds at f/16

Phacelia in early spring, near Chimneys, 55mm micro lens, 3 seconds at f/22

WILDFLOWERS

When isolating wildflowers, it is important to remember that surrounding foliage can be just as interesting as the flowers themselves. The greatest variation in the floral greens appears during spring. April, May and June are particularly outstanding months for shooting these plants, as their yellow- to blue-greens contrast sharply against the surrounding groundcovers. A 55mm or 105mm micro lens is commonly used for this approach to wildflower photography. A small aperture of f/22 or f/16 should suffice to secure enough depth of field for sharp images.

In composing shots, note carefully the position of flowers in the frame. For example, when photographing a scattering of wood sorrel blossoms and foliage, be sure the flowers don't pull your eye all over the frame; furthermore, don't cut the flowers in half by trying to fit too many into the photograph. Let this serve as a classic example of where simple composition works best.

While photographs of a single blossom can be spectacular, a close approach can be difficult. Isolating flowers means greater magnification of the subject, which, in turn, increases any movement of camera (by human vibration) or flower (by a breeze) and results in a blurred image. This is the time that true patience is tested. Under low-light situations, you may need to make a four-second (or longer) exposure, but be prepared to wait up to 20 or 30 minutes for the breeze to die down first.

Background may prove one of the most important elements in the final image. For example, sunlight reflecting on leaves can result in distractingly bright, out-of-focus highlights, and reflective pine needles can register as confusing lines crisscrossing the frame.

One practical solution is to shade the background with a white umbrella; white will not affect other colors but will permit neutral-colored diffused light to cover the subject area. Of course, the umbrella can also be used to shade both flower and background on a harshly lit sunny day.

When single flowers are photographed in the sun or shade, a shadow or dark area may look better if illuminated more. Mirrors provide a solution to this problem. When photographing flowers on a sunny day, two mirrors are ideal—one for backlighting the subject, the other for frontlighting. A mirror placed directly under the flower can reflect light into areas that otherwise would not be illuminated.

To control background even more, consider using a 200mm macro lens or an 80-200mm zoom lens with a bellows. The angle of coverage will be more restricted than with shorter focal-length lenses, but the decreased depth of field will place any annoying background out of focus.

Columbine, near Tremont, 80-200mm lens with bellows, 2 mirrors, 1/2 second at f/11

The aperture needed will be determined by the following: size of the flower (large flowers with significant depth need to be more in focus, so greater depth of field is required); distance from the background; and amount of magnification. Remember, the higher the magnification, the less depth of field.

Since a wide-angle lens has the ability to take in a large area, including hot spots and shadows, this lens works best on overcast days. Using a wide-angle lens enables you not only to photograph the wildflowers, but also to record their immediate environment.

Wide-angle lenses work well on flowers that grow in clusters, or ones that cover entire hillsides, such as fringed phacelia. The lens should be placed as close to the flowers as possible, and the aperture stopped down as far as the lens will allow for maximum depth of field. It is important that the subject closest to you be in sharp focus, with the background as sharp as the stopped-down lens will permit.

If you find yourself low to the ground, this might be a good time to consider using a right-angle viewfinder with a built-in eye cup. This simple attachment not only keeps you from smudging your face in the dirt, but it also protects surrounding flowers from being flattened by the sprawling photographer.

Crested dwarf iris, Greenbrier, 55mm micro lens, 1 second at f/22

Showy orchis, Bud Ogle Nature Trail, 55mm micro lens, 6 seconds at f/22

WILDFLOWER LOCATION GUIDE

WILDFLOWER	LOCATION	TIME
Bird-foot Violet	Bud Ogle Nature Trail	March-June
Bishop's Cap	Bud Ogle Nature Trail Roaring Fork Motor Nature Trail	April-June
Bleeding Heart	Little River Road	April-June

WILDFLOWER	LOCATION	TIME
Bloodroot	Cove Hardwood Trail	March-April
Bluets	Bud Ogle Nature Trail Deep Creek Area Little River Road Spruce-Fir Nature Trail	April-June
Canada Violet	Bud Ogle Nature Trail Chimneys Picnic Area	April-June
Carolina Rhododendron	Mount LeConte	June-July
Catawba Rhododendron	Alum Cave Bluff Trail Gregory Bald Maddron Bald Roaring Fork Motor Nature Trail	June-July
Catesby's Trillium	Cades Cove Nature Trail	April-May
Columbine	Little River Road	April-May
Common Blue Violet	Chimneys Picnic Area	March-June
Common Strawberry Crested Dwarf Iris	Bud Ogle Nature Trail Ash Hopper Trail Bud Ogle Nature Trail Greenbrier Cove	April-June April-May
Cut-leaved Toothwort	Bud Ogle Nature Trail	April-May
Ditch Stonecrop	Chimneys Picnic Area	April-July
Downy Yellow Violet	Bud Ogle Nature Trail	May-June
Dutchman's Breeches	Bud Ogle Nature Trail Chimneys Picnic Area	April-May
False Solomon's Seal	Chimneys Picnic Area Bud Ogle Nature Trail Deep Creek	May-July
Fire Pink	Little River Road Indian Creek Falls Trail	April-June
Flame Azalea	Andrews Bald Gregory Bald	May-June
Foamflower	Bud Ogle Nature Trail Chimneys Picnic Area	April-June
Gaywings	Abrams Falls Trail	April-June

WILDFLOWER	LOCATION	TIME
Great Chickweed	Little River Road Roaring Fork Motor Nature Trail	April-July
Greek Valerian	Bud Ogle Nature Trail	April-June
Indian Pipe	Abrams Falls Road Cades Cove Loop Road	June-September
Jack-in-the-Pulpit	Bud Ogle Nature Trail Chimneys Picnic Area Deep Creek Ephraim Bales Homestead	April-June
Jacob's Ladder	Bud Ogle Nature Trail	June-July
Ladies' Tresses	Rich Mountain Road Laurel Falls Trail	October-November
Large-flowered Trillium	Bud Ogle Nature Trail Cove Hardwoods Nature Trail Ephraim Bales Homestead	April-June
Long-spurred Violet	Bud Ogle Nature Trail	March-July
Mayapple	Cades Cove	April-June
Mountain Laurel	Alum Cave Bluff Trail Abrams Falls Trail Roaring Fork Motor Nature Trail	May-July
Painted Trillium	Clingmans Dome Mount LeConte	April-June
Passion Flower	Cades Cove	June-September
Pink Lady's Slipper	Bud Ogle Nature Trail Cades Cove Vista Nature Trail	April-June
Purple Fringed Orchid	Clingmans Dome Parking Area	June-Aug.
Purple Wake-Robin	Spruce-Fir Nature Trail	April-June
Rosebud Orchid	Alum Cave Bluff Trail Cades Cove Nature Trail	May-July

WILDFLOWER	LOCATION	TIME
Sand Myrtle	Mount LeConte	May-July
Showy Orchis	Bud Ogle Nature Trail Ash Hopper Trail Ephraim Bales Homestead	April-June
Smooth Solomon's Seal	Deep Creek	April-June
Squirrel Corn	Chimneys Picnic Area	April-May
Trout Lily	Cove Hardwoods Nature Trail	March-June
Vasey's Trillium	Ash Hopper Trail	April-June
White Fringed Phacelia	Chimneys Picnic Area Cove Hardwoods Nature Trail	April-May
White Rhododendron	Alum Cave Bluff Trail Greenbrier Sugarlands	June-July
Wild Blue Phlox	Bud Ogle Nature Trail Hwy. 441 near Oconaluftee Visitor Center	April-June
Wild Geranium	Bud Ogle Nature Trail	April-June
Wild Ginger	Roaring Fork Motor Nature Trail	April-May
Wood Sorrel	Roaring Fork Motor Nature Trail Grotto Falls Trail	May-July
Yarrow	Clingmans Dome	June-Sept.
Yellow Clintonia	Clingmans Dome	May-July
Yellow Fringed Orchid	Cades Cove Nature Trail Laurel Falls Trail	July-August
Yellow Lady's Slipper	Ash Hopper Trail Thomas Ridge Trail	April-June
Yellow Trillium	Bud Ogle Nature Trail Chimneys Picnic Area Cove Hardwoods Nature Trail Ephraim Bales Homestead Smokemont	April-June

MUSHROOMS

After a heavy rain, mushrooms swell with water and push up through surrounding leaves. Most mushrooms prefer low-light areas, and those that grow in bright sunlight do not last long. Since many are short-lived, it's wise to photograph them when you see them; they may never look better. Mushrooms can usually be found growing on, or under, fallen trees, or among decaying leaves.

Mushrooms shot at a low angle, showing the cap, stalk and ground together, can make for a pleasing portrait. If there is surrounding foliage, try to include it too; if not, you may need to isolate the mushroom in your photograph.

Since most mushrooms grow in poor-light situations, long exposures may be required for sharp focus. Fortunately, most mushrooms do not move in the wind. But because of the low light, it may be necessary to use fill flash, mirrors or a reflector to add extra light to shadow areas.

FERNS

In early summer, the park's ferns exhibit a variety of rich new greens. Some appear quite electric in color, especially when photographed under a canopy of leaves (which acts as a natural filter).

While there are various ways to photograph ferns, the characteristic common to most is maximum depth of field to ensure sharpness. Since ferns are especially prone to movement from the wind, check in advance for any swaying that might occur when using long shutter speeds required with small f-stops.

To isolate individual ferns, use a 105mm or 55mm macro lens. Wide-angle lenses in the 24mm to 35mm range work well for recording larger areas covered with ferns if you stop down your lens for maximum depth of field.

Framing ferns in the midst of other foliage makes them stand out even more, but be sure the entire area is within the shade. As

Mushroom in foliage, Cosby, 105mm lens, 1 second at f/16

Ferns and violets, Elkmont, 105mm lens, 1 second at f/16

an alternative, photograph ferns on an overcast day. This will eliminate the common problem of overexposed areas where the sun has illuminated a few ferns, making them the unintentional center of attention.

The ideal time to photograph ferns is just after a good rain, when their color intensifies dramatically. Color intensity can also be heightened by using a color-compensating filter with a slight green cast, such as a CC G5 or CC G10 filter.

FERN LOCATION GUIDE

FERN	*LOCATION*
Climbing Fern	Little River Road
Filmy Fern	Meigs Falls Chestnut Top Trail
Maidenhair Fern	Little River Road Chestnut Top Trail Indian Creek Falls Trail
Maidenhair Spleenwort	Chestnut Top Trail
Mountain Spleenwort	Sinks Parking Area
Netted Chain Fern	Sinks Parking Area
Sensitive Fern	Sinks Parking Area
Walking Fern	Elkmont Parking Area

Fall ferns, Elkmont, 105mm lens, 3 seconds at f/22

LICHENS

Of all the conceivable photographic subjects in the park, lichens are surely the least noticed—and not without good reason. Lichens are so well camouflaged on tree trunks that they can be completely overlooked without a good downpour—exactly the time most visitors retreat.

After a rain, examine trees closely. In contrast to the darkened bark, the multi-colored lichens now stand out vividly and take on an almost abstract quality when viewed close up. A 55mm or 105mm micro lens works quite well here.

Look for patterns that merge, creating unique designs in your viewfinder. Stopping all the way down is essential to get all of a curving tree trunk in focus. The small aperture, together with the light lost on a rainy day, will require longer exposure times. Fortunately, only a terrific gust of wind can sway the larger lichen-covered trees.

Rock walls and boulders are also frequently covered with lichens, and, once again, it is the moisture here that brings out their colors. Look for a flower growing from a crevice in a rock wall covered with lichens; the contrast of colors and textures can be quite striking.

WILDLIFE

To the casual observer, the Smoky Mountains seldom reveal the wealth of wildlife native to the area. The national park is one of the last true strongholds in the East for the black bear, and it is also home to more species of salamanders than any other area in the world. In fact, the red-cheeked salamander lives nowhere else.

As in other Eastern forests, white-tailed deer live here, along with woodland mice, raccoons, opossums, skunks and dozens of other natives. Birds may be harder to spot; they are best located by first listening for their calls.

Because of an absence of open spaces, greater effort is required to photograph wildlife in the Smokies. Yet, for those who

Lichen and rust, along roadside near Newfound Gap, 55mm micro lens, 6 seconds at f/22

White-tailed deer, Cades Cove, 300mm lens, 1/125 second at f/4.5

Black bear, Cades Cove, 105mm lens, 1/60 second at f/4

are truly determined, a wide variety of species are available at all times of the year.

When deciding which equipment to use, it might be prudent to note that one of the most important features in a successful wildlife photograph is sharp focus on the eyes, even at the expense of the beak, snout or nose. To keep the eye in focus and to compose the exact image you want, you may find a motor drive is of great value.

BEARS

The black bear is the most popular and sought-after animal in the Smoky Mountains; a bear sighted along the roadside can back up cars for miles. Nevertheless,

exceptional photographs of black bears are rare.

For one thing, bears usually appear in low-light situations, making it difficult to shoot at a fast shutter speed with fine-grained film. Black bears also tend to keep their noses to the ground, rooting around for acorns and berries. When they do raise their heads, they are usually on the move. If you are lucky enough to see a bear climbing a tree, you should work quickly to capture it on film, because bears predictably climb out of view once they reach thick foliage.

A medium telephoto lens is strongly recommended both to keep a safe distance and to isolate the bear from its

background. One of the most dangerous situations in the park can develop if you attempt to photograph bear cubs: Be absolutely certain you do not come between the cubs and their mother.

In fact, it's a good idea to keep a safe distance from *all* bears. Many times, bears seem quite docile and ignore the curious tourists who have crowded around; still, you should remember they are aggressive animals that move quickly and need plenty of room.

If you see a bear out in the open, try to position yourself where you can shoot an out-of-focus background of green foliage. Alternately, try photographing a bear against a blue sky to make it stand out.

DEER

The largest population of white-tailed deer can be found in Cades Cove, where you are most likely to see them along the 11-mile loop in the early morning. Because these deer are shy, a lens with a focal length of at least 300mm will be required.

Like most wildlife, deer blend in well with their environment. This is yet another reason why a longer lens should be used. By shooting wide open, you will be able to separate them from the background. This is particularly important if the deer are too far off in the distance and you want to use them as one component of a landscape.

Deer graze in the open at first light. You can be ready for them by setting up your equipment on the edge of the woods, keeping yourself behind a tree or crouching behind low-growing foliage.

Because of the stream of noisy traffic, the deer tend to move from field to field. Trying to stalk these deer rarely works because of their keen sense of smell and hearing; it's best if you remain stationary and wait for them. Some of the deer in the park are relatively tame, so, with a little patience, even the most inexperienced photographer can usually obtain a good photograph.

Photographing deer in the woods, on the other hand, can be extremely difficult because of the low-light conditions and the many trees and branches that invariably seem to bisect the animal.

Consider this: Your car can make an excellent blind, since the deer are accustomed to the sight and sound of an automobile. To avoid vibrations, turn off the motor before photographing, and don't get out of the car if a deer wanders over in your direction. And remember, the Cades Cove Loop Road becomes quite busy after 10 a.m. on weekends.

White-tailed deer, Cades Cove, 300mm lens, 1/60 second at f/4.5

SMALL MAMMALS

Woodchucks, rabbits and squirrels can be found throughout the park, but they are most frequently seen in the Cades Cove area. Since these small mammals are far more shy than the park's bears or deer, you'll need a lens at least 300mm in focal length. A faster lens will allow a faster shutter speed, but the extra weight and bulk will require a tripod.

A low angle is effective when photographing these ground-level mammals. This, in conjunction with a wide aperture, will make the subject stand out against an out-of-focus background.

Woodchucks dig their holes in the middle of fields, and the slightest disturbance will send them running into their dens. If you use fill flash, you will alert the animals to your presence and probably scare them off. Shooting in the open allows plenty of light to illuminate the subject, although early-morning and late-afternoon light is best.

If you plan to follow woodchucks or other animals into the fields, be sure to bring an extra change of clothing, since the grasses are frequently wet and full of ticks.

BIRDS

Birds have so much cover in the Smoky Mountains that the only practical place to photograph them is near feeders set up by some of the lodges. Normally, birds feed more frequently in the morning and evening hours; they also feed more actively during nesting season.

Since, in general, birds are wary around people, you'll need a lens with a focal length of at least 300mm, usually shot wide open. A motor drive will also prove helpful for capturing the many poses and behavioral displays that materialize so quickly.

A motor drive is also essential when photographing birds in flight. You won't have time to take a meter reading, focus and shoot while composing the subject. It's much easier to take a meter reading and set your camera in advance (preferably at 1/500 or 1/1000 second). Then, when the subject flies by, simply focus and shoot several frames while panning. If using this approach, remember to follow

Young raccoons, Cades Cove, 80-200mm lens, 1 flash, 1/60 second at f/4.5

through and continue the panning motion even after you have taken the photograph.

If you wish to capture a highlight in the eye or a detail in the darker feathers, you may need a fill flash. But do not use your flash as the main light source. Not only will the bird be lit against a black background, but, because of the combination of a relatively slow flash-synchronization speed and quick movements of the bird, ghosting will commonly result (i.e., a sharp image will be created by the flash, with a fuzzy outline from ambient light).

FROGS

Frogs are best photographed at night. One workable setup for illuminating the subject is that described in the section on nocturnal photography, but without the red acetate filter. Frogs and toads are mesmerized by a bright shaft of light, so photographing them is easier than most other nocturnal animals. Light, however, can affect their behavior. Should this happen, adjust the light source so it illuminates the area adjacent to the frog, while still providing sufficient light to focus on your subject. Normal behavior will usually ensue.

Frogs are commonly found in the vicinity of streams and ponds, and they can be located by their calls. By mimicking their mating calls or playing an audio tape of frog calls, you can attract more frogs and make the males more vocal, expediting your efforts to locate them.

An 80-200mm zoom lens mounted on a bellows, or a 200mm macro lens, is the best equipment for shooting frogs. Also, two flash units, one mounted on each side of the camera, may prove helpful.

SALAMANDERS

To the majority of visitors, perhaps the least-known inhabitants of the park are the 23 different species of salamanders. Because of their small size and chiefly nocturnal habits, these amphibians are rarely noticed. Salamanders generally can be found under rocks and logs or in streams. They are more readily found at night, especially during or after a rain, when they travel in search of food.

Like other wildlife, salamanders require much greater patience and determination than shooting landscapes. A close-up device is required, such as a 105mm or 200mm macro lens, or a standard lens with extension. When photographing salamanders in close-up, it is not always advisable to shoot the entire body. Sometimes the front third of the body, with the head up and not buried in mud or mosses, can be more revealing; so, too, is a salamander with his back arched—a sure sign the salamander is alarmed—as a demonstration of natural behavior. When shooting, you will find low angles

Gray treefrog, Sugarlands, 80-200mm lens with bellows, 2 flash units, 1/60 second at f/11

Red-cheeked salamander, Spruce-Fir Nature Trail, 55mm micro lens, 1 second at f/16

isolate salamanders from their backgrounds quite effectively.

For night photography, a flashlight and two flash units will be needed. Mounting one flash unit onto a bracket off each side of the camera will eliminate harsh shadows. And mounting a small flashlight on a monoball head attached to the camera flash mount will enable you to see the subject more clearly.

At first, salamanders appear to be slow-moving, on cool nights especially. But beware: If you turn your back for even an instant, the salamander may dart underground or slip under some debris.

The red-cheeked (or Appalachian woodland) salamander lives nowhere else in the world outside of the Smoky Mountains. For this reason, special care should be taken when photographing these small animals.

SNAKES AND LIZARDS
Photographing snakes and lizards is best done from a distance, not only for safety considerations, but also because they are easily frightened away. These reptiles are hard to find, although you will have your best luck hunting them in the summer months.

Skinks and fence lizards like to warm themselves by basking in the sun. If you move in close, you can usually get good photographs because they tend to remain motionless while sunning. A 105mm or 200mm macro lens, or an 80-200mm zoom lens on a tripod, works well in this situation; try to get down on their level, even if it means getting flat on your stomach.

Snakes, on the other hand, are not as cooperative as lizards, and it's not a good idea to be flat on your stomach close to a snake. In the Smokies, it is nearly impossible to find snakes moving through the underbrush. Many lie coiled in the early morning, still lethargic from the cool mountain nights. At this time, you can use a longer exposure to gain depth of field if you have a sturdy tripod.

Usually, however, photographing snakes requires use of flash units, especially if you

Fence lizard, Cades Cove, 80-200mm lens with bellows, 2 mirrors, 1/4 second at f/11

want a shot of a tongue flicked out. (Since snakes have a highly developed sense of heat and smell, you may prompt one to flick its tongue by blowing your warm breath in its direction.)

Remember, however, that two poisonous species of snakes are native to the park: copperheads and rattlesnakes.

INSECTS

Insect photography requires special equipment and some unique approaches. Some sort of macro device is definitely required—a 105mm or 200mm macro lens, or an 80-200mm lens mounted on a bellows, works best.

At the magnification necessary to photograph most insects, there will be little depth of field. To get as sharp a focus as possible, it is important to line up the film plane parallel to the subject. This often will require some unusually low camera positions and a sturdy tripod spread out at ground level.

Insects that are fairly stationary can be illuminated with mirrors. Species that move constantly, however, may require a flash (or two flashes, to eliminate shadows).

Although all insects eat, mate and (some) fly, it is hard to photograph insect activities. Some, such as ants, carry out complex social functions. Capturing their activities on film requires working with anywhere from 3x to 7x magnification, thus necessitating the use of flash.

On early fall mornings, many insects, including butterflies, are cold and covered with dew, waiting for the first sunlight to warm them. This is an ideal time to photograph them. Butterflies approached slowly will usually remain still. Occasionally one will fly off, but you will discover that if you wait motionless, it will soon return to the very same flower.

SPIDERS

Spiders are easy to photograph, since they usually wait perfectly still for their prey or are busy wrapping their victims with silk. Again, a macro system of some sort is needed, and a mirror to reflect light (or a flash to stop action) is helpful.

Buckeye butterfly, Cades Cove, 80-200mm lens with bellows, 2 mirrors, 1/4 second at f/11

Sun and spiderweb, near Oconaluftee, 80-200mm lens with bellows, 1/30 second at f/4.5

The 80-200mm zoom lens mounted on a bellows provides a good system for shooting spiders, especially if the web is attached to grasses that might be disturbed if you were to move closer. The magnification can be changed without altering your position simply by extending the bellows. Be sure to work off a stable tripod, and always use a cable release.

Spider webs covered with dew in the early morning can be dramatic—especially when backlit. If you align the film plane parallel with the web, you won't need to stop the lens all the way down, thus permitting you to shoot at a faster speed and keep the background out of focus. If you find the background is in bright sunlight and out-of-focus highlights intrude, you may wish to consider shading the background with an umbrella or dark-colored coat. Using this technique, you may need to underexpose from the setting your meter indicates by up to as many as two f-stops.

Aligning a rising or setting sun with a spider spinning a web—or with a web only—can also be quite dramatic. Once again, it is important to line up the film plane parallel to the web and to shoot with the aperture wide open to ensure a round-shaped sun.

SALAMANDER HABITAT GUIDE

SALAMANDER	HABITAT
Appalachian Seal	Boggy spots, streams
Black-bellied	Larger streams 1,150-6,000 feet
Black-chinned Red	Under rocks, logs
Blue Ridge Mountain	Moist to saturated locations Clingmans Dome to 1,100 feet
Blue Ridge Spring	Throughout the park
Blue Ridge Two-lined	Near springs 2,000 feet and up
Four-toed	Sphagnum or boggy locations
Hellbender	Large streams with shelter Below 2,100 feet
Long-tailed	Under logs and rocks Tennessee side of park
Marbled	Low altitudes Cades Cove, Laurel Creek
Metcalf's	Chestnut-oak forest under logs 3,500-5,800 feet Balsam Mountain area
Midland Mud	Muddy streams
Mudpuppy	Lowest altitude (850-1,000 feet) Abrams Creek (Rare in park)
Pygmy	4,000 feet to mountain summits
Red-backed	Up to 5,500 feet
Red-cheeked	Clingmans Dome to 2,800 feet
Red-spotted Newt	Cades Cove
Shovel-nosed	Small brooks under stones Above 1,500 feet
Slimy	Common in lower altitudes
Spotted	Woodland ponds
Three-lined	Springs and ponds North Carolina side of park
Zigzag	Rockslides or near cave mouths Below 2,500 feet Tennessee side of park

SUNRISE AND SUNSET

The Clingmans Dome and Newfound Gap areas are two of the most popular locations for photographing sunrises and sunsets. It takes roughly 30 minutes to drive from Gatlinburg or Cherokee to the top of the mountain, so an early start is essential.

The colors begin 30 to 40 minutes before the sun comes into view. Oranges and yellows on the horizon stand out in stark contrast to the brilliant blue. During this period of time, exposures anywhere from 1/2 second to 10 seconds may be required, according to how clear a day it is. About 10 to 15 minutes before the sun rises, the sky usually becomes gray and washed out—not a good time to photograph.

As the sun comes into view, the camera meter will register false readings. However, by metering off to the side of the sun and underexposing 1/2 to 1 f-stop, a proper exposure should be realized.

Employ the same metering techniques on sunsets. Just as at sunrise, there will be a period of brilliant color, this time 20 to 40 minutes after sunset. These colors depend on weather and vary from day to day.

When a camera points into the sun, lens flare can be a problem. To minimize flare, use a lens shade and avoid a filter unless absolutely necessary. Never look at the sun through a viewfinder for long periods of time, and do not leave your camera pointed at the sun after you've finished shooting.

A lens in the range of 80 to 200mm, or even a 300mm lens, works well if you wish to include the layered mountains and the sun just as it rises or sets. A wider-angle lens usually captures too much foreground and sky, which detracts from the photograph. Unlike in areas where air pollution abounds or where the sun rises and sets over vast areas of flat land, a 300mm lens used in these mountains will not cause the sun to dominate the photograph.

It is not always essential to include the sun in a photograph when shooting sunrises and sunsets. Framing off to the side of the sun, and including a small amount of sky with the mountains, can add color that does not exist at midday.

Layering mountains at sunset, Clingmans Dome, 300mm lens, 1/250 second at f/5.6

GUIDE to SUNRISES and SUNSETS

LOCATION	DESCRIPTION
SUNRISE	
Andrews Bald	The sun often rises through low-lying clouds and fog drifting over the mountain ridges below.
Clingmans Dome Parking Lot	The sun rising over the layered mountains may be viewed from the east end. This classic view is not obscured by foliage.
Clingmans Dome Road Pulloff	The sun rises over a dominant ridge, with the view unobstructed. The pulloff (about 4 miles from the parking lot) only holds 2 to 3 cars.
Myrtle Point	This is an open area with the sun rising over a fine view of layered mountains.
Newfound Gap Overlook	The sun frequently rises through the fog. Ridges in the foreground can be silhouetted for contrast.
SUNSET	
Clifftop	There are many vantage points from which you can shoot the sun setting behind silhouetted trees.
Clingmans Dome Parking Lot	A fine sunset may be viewed from the boulders at the west end of the parking lot. There are no trees to obscure this frequently colorful sunset.
Morton Overlook	The classic view of sunset—an orange-colored sun setting over pastel mountains—can be photographed from this unobstructed view.

Fall foliage, Sugarlands, 80-200mm lens, 1 second at f/16

FALL COLOR

The peak time for fall color varies, but, on average, the foliage is most dramatic from Oct. 16 to 25. Because of variations in elevation, the colors begin changing on the tops of mountains first, then work their way down to the foothills.

The dominant color for fall in the Smoky Mountains is yellow, with brown, crimson and orange interspersed. Pulloffs all along the road from Gatlinburg to Cherokee offer wide vistas of spectacular color.

If you hike the park's trails, you will discover that water reflects the colors of leaves hanging overhead. Streams can look like molten gold as they reflect the bright yellows of poplars. The faster the water moves, the more the different colors will mix together and lose their brilliance. For this reason, exposures should not exceed 1/15 second.

Autumn color is at its richest during or right after a rain, although downpours will knock leaves to the ground and into streams. Many successful autumn-color photographs are of leaves strewn across moss-covered boulders, or of leaves lining the banks of a fast-running stream.

It is better to isolate areas of color than to try to take in an entire mountainside where there is no center of interest. Stop your lens down to f/16 or f/22 to achieve maximum depth of field; not only will the foreground trees be in focus, but also the background trees.

Trees with colorful fall leaves set against dark conifers as background make for powerful photographs. The sharp contrast makes the leaves stand out more than against a blue sky. In fact, unless blue sky adds to the fall color—which it seldom does—it's best not to include it at all. Frequently it only draws attention away from the foliage.

Some people feel that the more brilliantly colored leaves you can squeeze into a photograph, the better it will be. This is simply not true. Some photographs are so cluttered with color that there is no place to rest the eye. It is far better to select an area with a rich mix of colors—red, yellow,

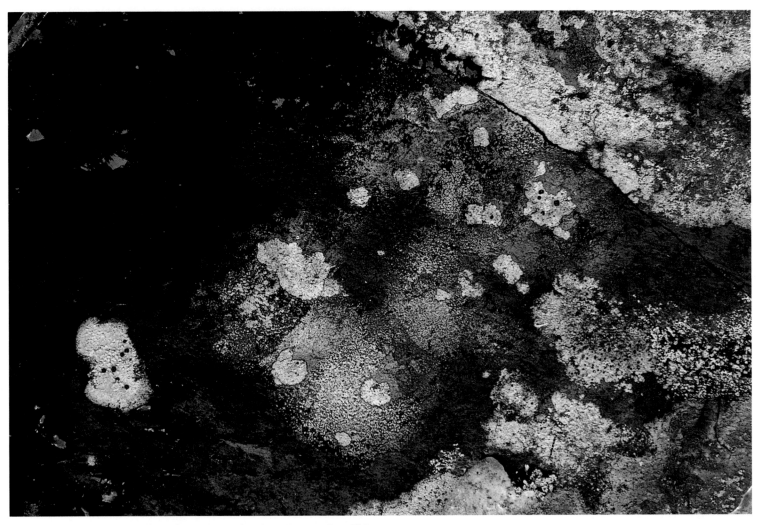

Lichens and rust, near Newfound Gap, 55mm micro lens, 3 seconds at f/22

brown and, especially, gray leaves. This is also the time of year that a green leaf will almost jump right out at you.

Leaves covered with frost are also quite dramatic, especially when the early-morning sun strikes them. But except for the coldest of mornings, when the sun illuminates the frost, it also melts it, so you must work quickly.

Cades Cove is a fine location for shooting treelines in autumn and for isolating individual trees. Here, you can work without limbs from other trees interfering with your composition, which they often do in the middle of the woods.

ABSTRACTS

Photographers are always abstracting—isolating one area from an infinite number of others, deciding which elements of a scene convey the message intended at that moment in time. Abstracting need not be obscure or unrecognizable; subjects are sometimes isolated and magnified to the point where an object almost breaks from reality.

In the Smokies, lichens growing on the face of rock walls provide an excellent subject for creating abstracts. Their colorful patterns can even take on the look of a modern artist's canvas. Since there is no

movement among these subjects, even under conditions of very low light, long exposures that provide great depth of field can be used.

Ice, too, creates patterns and distorts reality. It can be transparent or opaque, and it may reflect the deep blues of the sky above. If you choose to photograph ice frozen on steep rock walls, beware of those shimmering icicles hanging overhead: The larger ones are potentially dangerous, especially on a warm day.

Finally, note too that tree bark can assume interesting patterns—especially sycamore bark, with its motley array of greens, whites, grays and browns.

CADES COVE

Perhaps the most popular area to visit in the park is Cades Cove. The main road is a one-way loop about 11 miles long, usually congested with heavy traffic on weekends. On Saturday mornings during the summer, the road is closed to cars, and bicycles may be rented at the campground store near the beginning of the loop. The road passes beside large open fields and hardwood forests, where wildlife forage and wildflowers and mushrooms grow undisturbed, and beside the old churches and homesteads of settlers of the original Cades Cove community, founded in the early 1800s. A picnic area and campground (open year-round) are provided.

Open meadows, especially the first two on the left-hand side of the road, are grazing fields for cattle and horses belonging to local farmers. At daybreak, however, deer are regularly seen grazing in these same meadows; often they number as many as a dozen. When conditions are right, the deer are surrounded by fog, frost or snow, making for a picturesque setting.

Just beyond the fields, on the right, is a densely wooded and hilly area. Wild turkeys, though hard to find, roam here. Black bears are not uncommon, although an encounter with one is not an everyday experience. Wild boars (descended from the livestock of the first settlers) also abound in these woods. They are rarely seen, but their paths of destruction are easy to recognize.

The main road passes several old rural churches and their adjoining cemeteries. These are frequent stops for park visitors (and one reason the traffic is so slow). The white wood buildings and simple architectural styles provide for popular and photogenic subjects, especially when surrounded by vivid fall foliage. One fine

Bloodroot, Cades Cove, 80-200mm lens with bellows, 2 mirrors, 1 second at f/16

view of a church in autumn is from Rich Mountain Road, where you can see the church in the valley below, nestled in fall colors.

The major tourist attraction on the loop road is the **John Cable Mill,** which includes a cantilevered barn, visitor center and an assortment of other buildings. The mill (an authentic waterwheel) still operates April through October, and freshly milled corn can be purchased here. The area affords a welcome place for a peaceful walk, especially along the adjoining stream.

Many **sugar maples** and **sweet gum** trees stand on the edge of the clearing, making for spectacular fall color. The main house is situated behind an old wooden fence, with multilayered mountains rising in the background, sometimes partially obscured by fog. Less than one-half mile from the parking area is the **Cades Cove Nature Trail,** only about one-third mile round trip and home to **Catesby's trillium, yellow-fringed orchid** and **rosebud orchid.**

Other appealing stops that offer a glimpse of how the early settlers lived are the John Oliver place, one of the first stops on the loop road, and the Elijah Oliver place, by the Abrams Falls trail. These log cabins remain unspoiled, and the craftsmanship is still apparent.

Cades Cove offers many other enticements besides the obvious tourist stops. As noted, this is a prime location to view wildlife. From the first fields along the loop, **white-tailed deer** graze until one or two hours past dawn. Since the fields are quite large, the deer can see you every step of the way and hence are less likely to be startled. If you are careful, you can even approach them (to what they consider a safe distance) for a photograph.

Black bears are far less common, but they like to forage in the woods off to the right as you drive along the loop. You'll often see them crossing the road or prowling the hollows in the woods. Be extremely careful, however; never approach them. While they may move slowly much of the time, they can be surprisingly fast when it suits them.

Wild turkeys and **wild boars** are not ordinarily visible here, but, if you are lucky, you might glimpse one off to the right in the woods, especially near the beginning of the loop.

A more commonplace animal, though frequently overlooked, is the **groundhog.** The best place to see them is in the vicinity of the old homestead cabins by some of the pulloffs. A little patience is required here. Groundhogs will not come to trust you, but they are reasonably tolerant, and you may be lucky enough to snap a photograph.

Wildflowers can be found in the woods all along the loop. This is one of the best areas for **Indian pipe,** which can also be found along the gravel road leading to the Primitive Baptist Church. This is also a particularly good place to locate **mayapples,** whose broad leaves hide their beautiful flowers from most visitors. **Morels** (large fungi) also abound here, as well as a seemingly infinite number of mushrooms.

Several roads are accessible from the Cades Cove Loop Road. Rich Mountain Road was once an Indian trail. This road intersects the loop road at the Missionary Baptist Church and ends in Townsend, Tenn. Along the way, you'll pass through Tuckaleechee Cove and have several good opportunities to photograph backlit leaves as you drive through the forest. **Black bears** can also be seen roaming the woods here.

Several clearings along the road provide excellent views of the cove and the valleys below. Although this was the first major route into Cades Cove in the early 1800s, there is very little traffic today. Parson Branch Road is an 8-mile one-way road that begins just past the Cable Mill pulloff. The road passes through a forest of hemlock and poplar, and in the spring you'll be able to see **catawba rhododendron** in bloom.

The one waterfall in Cades Cove is **Abrams Falls,** named for the Cherokee chief who assumed the English name "Abram." The trail to the falls begins in the Abrams Falls parking area, just past the Abrams Creek bridge on the loop road. The walk to the falls is 5 miles round trip and definitely worthwhile for the views and flora—like the **gaywings** and **Indian pipe**—along the way, and for the 20-foot falls at the end. In the spring, **mountain laurel** bloom along many parts of the trail.

Gregory Bald hosts **catawba rhododendron** and is regarded by many as home to the world's greatest display of **flame azaleas.** A grass bald, its best stands of azaleas are found along the edges.

Two trails lead to Gregory Bald. Forge Creek Road, which begins at the Cable Mill, intersects Gregory Ridge Trail; Hannah Mountain Trail intersects Parson Branch Road at Sam's Gap. Be advised that the shortest possible hike to Gregory Bald is about 9 miles, so check with the park rangers in advance to be sure the azaleas are in bloom. Also inquire about the demands of each trail, and don't forget to ask whether the road where you park your car will still be open when you return.

CHIMNEYS PICNIC AREA

The Chimneys picnic area off the road to Newfound Gap (Highway 441) consists of picnic tables, cooking grills and restrooms. In early to mid-April, however, it is transformed into a seemingly endless garden of wildflowers. One of the ideal features of this area is that it requires no walking to see the display of color, since the flowers are right off the roadside as you enter. There is also a trail along the back edge of the hillside, and it continues on up to yet more wildflowers.

The most densely blooming wildflower area is the hillside to the right as you enter the parking area. In April, it is a sea of **white-fringed phacelia,** so thick it looks like freshly fallen snow. **Yellow trillium** are often found with phacelia, and, in the Chimneys picnic area, the two largest stands are just off the roadside as you enter the parking lot and around the bend of the hillside facing the parking area.

Mixed in with the phacelia are **false Solomon's seal, foamflower, common blue violet, Canada violet** and **Jack-in-the-pulpit,** especially in the area just off the roadside. In early spring, **Dutchman's breeches** and heart-shaped **squirrel corn** can be found throughout the hillside. Solitary waxy-white **large-flowered trillium** and **ditch stonecrop** are also quite common.

The Chimneys picnic area is the trailhead for the **Cove Hardwood Nature Trail,** which hosts **trout lily, white-fringed phacelia, yellow trillium** and **large-flowered trillium** and passes through large stands of hemlock. The trail loop is less than a mile long, and a self-guiding leaflet is available in boxes at the trailhead. A variety of flowering trees, including **silverbell, black locust** and **yellowwood,** can be seen along this trail.

Dutchman's breeches, Chimneys Picnic Area, 55mm micro lens, 1 second at f/22

CLINGMANS DOME/NEW-FOUND GAP

Widely known for their vistas and fog-shrouded mountains, the tourist stops at Clingmans Dome and Newfound Gap are among the most popular in the park. Located on the road from Gatlinburg to Cherokee, the Newfound Gap parking area on the Tennessee-North Carolina border overlooks the valley below.

The 7-mile road to the Clingmans Dome parking lot is several hundred yards away from the Newfound Gap parking area (on the main road); it brings you to one of the most spectacular (and most easily accessible) overlooks of the park. Because of the high elevations, both locations are considerably cooler than the rest of the park, particularly in early morning.

Newfound Gap, 15 miles from Gatlinburg, is an excellent place to photograph **sunrises.** On clear days, the sky to the left of the valley can light up with color about 30 to 45 minutes before sunrise. The treelines, standing out as silhouettes, provide fine composition at this time of day.

The area is frequently covered in fog in early morning, however, and the predawn sky is not always visible. This is an ideal time to photograph the treelines in the **fog**—particularly as the fog lifts from the nearby mountains. Thus, instead of a harsh sunrise, the fog serves to soften the sun as it rises in the sky, and you'll be able to photograph it against the silhouettes of fog-shrouded treelines.

It's not uncommon for the fog to continue to roll in and out for several hours, and this will provide you with an almost endless variety of photographic opportunities. In the fall, the foliage in the foreground in the fog is also striking.

Clingmans Dome, named for a North Carolina Civil War hero and senator, Thomas Clingman, is also a good place to view sunrises. During the summer months, position yourself at the east end of the parking lot to photograph the sun rising over the mountains in the distance.

An even better location for this, however, is from the pulloffs along the road to Clingmans Dome. At these early hours, the parking lot is an ideal spot for photographing the **layering of the mountains** and the fog in the valleys between them. You will see firsthand why the park is called the "Smokies." Fog appears quite frequently, although commonly it's a fine mist.

This is a good opportunity to walk back along the trail toward the restrooms and photograph the **mountain ash** and other trees in this luminescent fog. Incidentally, while the lookout tower once was a fine observation point, the surrounding trees have grown so tall over the years that most views are obstructed. It's a nice walk one-half mile uphill, but you'll do much better photographing from the parking lot: **sunrise** from the east side in summer, layering of the mountains facing southeast, and **sunset** from the rocks on the west end.

Because of heavy moisture provided by the fog, Clingmans Dome is an excellent area to photograph **mosses** and **lichens.** In late spring and summer, the parking area is also full of wildflowers, although the higher elevation causes them to bloom later than you might expect. Among some of the more common are **purple-fringed orchid, yarrow,** crimson **bee balm,** pink **turtlehead** and dark blue **closed gentian.**

Many trails lead from the parking lot and road to it. In the early morning, you may be lucky enough to see bobcat or red fox crossing the road or trails. These trails are generally bordered with lush ferns, particularly **marginal shield ferns,** and a variety of wildflowers, including **painted trillium, bluets** and **yellow clintonia.**

One of the shortest trails—and perhaps most representative—is the **Spruce-Fir Nature Trail.** It is only about one-half mile round trip and can be located roughly 3 miles from the road's intersection with Newfound Gap Road. Because of the high altitude, this trail affords the opportunity to experience a forest usually only encountered much farther north.

The hiking trail to **Andrews Bald** begins at the Clingmans Dome parking area. It is only 4 miles, round trip, and passes by a fine stand of **flame azaleas** that bloom in June.

Layering mountains, Clingmans Dome, 80-200mm lens, 1 second at f/11

Mountain stream, Cosby, 28mm lens, 3 seconds at f/16

COSBY

The Cosby area is one of the few places in the park that is both easily accessible and secluded. Just off U.S. Highway 321 past Greenbrier, it consists of a picnic area and campground adjoining a fast-moving stream.

The area is virtually blanketed with ferns, mostly **marginal shield ferns**. On either side of the stream are clusters of mushrooms that may be found at almost any time of year as a result of the high humidity. The rocks alongside and in the stream are covered with **mosses**, and many trees are festooned with **lichens**. For the amateur naturalist who wishes to stay near the parking/picnic area and campground, it's hard to beat the Cosby area of the park.

Near the Cosby campground amphitheater is the trailhead for the **Cosby Nature Trail**. It's only about three-fourths of a mile round trip, and in the spring it is particularly striking when the wildflowers and the delicate and fragrant **partridgeberry** abound. **Maddron Bald** can also be reached by trail from Cosby. The 5-mile hike (one-way) passes by an abundance of **catawba rhododendron** and **blueberry** bushes along the **Snake Den Mountain Trail**, which hikers can pick up at the Cosby campground. It's tough climbing until it reaches **Indian Camp Creek Trail**, one-half mile from the Bald.

The trail to **Hen Wallow Falls**, only 4 miles round trip, passes by some of the largest trees in the park; this trail, too, begins at the Cosby campground. You can also reach **Mount Cammerer** by way of **Low Gap Trail** from the campground. It's about 11 miles round trip, almost all of it uphill. The tower on Mount Cammerer provides for some magnificent views of the park. At lower elevations, the trail is rich with **rhododendron**, both red and white, which give way to the **birch, hemlocks, spruces** and **firs** of the higher elevations at trail's end.

DEEP CREEK

Because of the length of the drive (up to two hours because of the slow-moving traffic) from the park through Cherokee and Bryson City, N.C., to Deep Creek, this area is not used as much as others. However, it does offer a rich variety of attractions —including a mountain stream, three waterfalls and horse trails—making it a worthwhile trip.

The parking lot, just beyond the campground, is adjacent to Deep Creek. Along the banks of the stream are several stands of **bluets**. As you face the stream, one stand can be found about even with the center of the lot; the other is about 50 yards to the right. Both stands grow against the moist rocks along the water's edge. Small eddies along the edge, and the backwash from each, also make for interesting patterns. Numerous rocks break the surface of the stream in the middle, and the patterns created as water rushes past are highly photogenic.

The far side of the stream is covered with **catawba rhododendron** and **mountain laurel** foliage, usually in deep shade. However, this provides a backdrop to the leaves of the more brightly lit foliage hanging over the stream. Many photographs of the rushing stream and backlit foliage or autumnal foliage against the dark background are possible from the near shore. **Juneywhank Falls**, a 1.5-mile round-trip walk from the parking lot, is not as spectacular as other attractions in this area of the park.

The main trail follows the water upstream to higher elevations. This provides an excellent opportunity to photograph a mountain stream from a higher vantage point, showing it in relation to its surroundings. It also provides an opportunity to photograph a stream through the trees— which is especially effective while the trees are still full of fall's colors.

Along the way, the stream passes over some large moss-covered boulders, and there are also thick stands of **marginal shield ferns** and red **hearts-a-bustin'**.

Mountain stream, Deep Creek, 28mm lens, 3 seconds at f/16

Solomon's seal, false Solomon's seal, fire pink, Jack-in-the-pulpit, white flowering dogwood, lobelia and **cardinal flower** are some of the numerous other species of plants you may see at different times of the year along the trail.

Tom's Branch Falls is only a quarter mile from the Deep Creek parking lot. The water winds its way 60 feet down the mountain, skimming across the rocks as it falls to the stream. The upper part of the falls is neither impressive nor photogenic, in part because it is chiefly hidden by the thick foliage, and also because high contrast as the light filters through the canopy creates bright spots all along the upper area of the falls.

The area where the water hits the creek is far more suitable as a photographic subject. The lighting here is usually very even, and the rushing water creates white silky patterns as it covers the rocks at the bottom. Numerous trees on the near side of the stream may be used for framing the falls, and there is sufficient cleared area to photograph it in a variety of ways.

As you continue hiking upstream, the trail

makes a right-hand turn and passes over a bridge, then continues on to the left. Just past the bridge are two areas (to the left) worth examining. In both, the stream and trail are again at the same level, and you can achieve fine composition of the stream with surrounding foliage. The trail begins a climb uphill next, where once again you can see the stream below.

The trail levels off before Indian Creek Falls, but just before that a trail veers off to the left where a wooden bridge crosses the creek. The bridge is an ideal place to photograph the stream in the midst of a **catawba rhododendron** and **mountain laurel** thicket, but beware of vibrations from the bridge.

Indian Creek Falls is only a few hundred yards farther along the main trail. A rest stop and bench are provided, and there is a short path down to the pool at the base of the 40-foot falls. When there is much water flowing, it is highly photogenic.

This area also seems to attract many butterflies, perhaps because of the cool breezes. They're usually on the ground to the left of the clearing by the pool, and may be approached with care.

GREENBRIER

Named for the vine with heart-shaped leaves and thorns that clings to the rocks, the Greenbrier area of the park has an entrance on U.S. Highway 321, 6 miles outside (east) of Gatlinburg. A dirt road follows the Middle Prong of the Little Pigeon River, and it is the trailhead for a number of long hiking trails (the trail to Ramsay Cascades is one of the more popular). The area is not heavily frequented, yet it provides for some of the best photographic experiences in the park.

The dirt road is always above the level of the stream, yet it is an easy task to get to the water's edge. Toward the beginning of the road, the stream passes over some rather unusually shaped rocks—for the most part flat and very pitted. These rocks are large enough to stand on, fortunately, and photographing the stream from a very low angle with a wide-angle lens will include the **pitted rocks**, rushing water and a few cascades in the distance.

As the road continues, different views of the stream are afforded, almost all of them photogenic, especially when the **white rhododendron** blooms. The road eventually makes a left-hand turn over a wooden bridge; three photographic opportunities of the **stream** are available here.

First, the stream can be photographed through the trees (this is especially effective when the fall foliage is colorful or when the greens of spring are still new). As you move along the edge of the road, you will see an endless variety of scenes of rushing white water through the foliage. Two smaller streams converge to form the main stream here, adding to the variety of options.

Next, the stream can be photographed from water level. There are enough large rocks to frame in the foreground, with foliage along the sides and background,

Stream after summer rains, Greenbrier, 28mm lens, 6 seconds at f/16

to create an image of a mountain stream lost in the depths of the forest. This is especially effective with fall foliage, or when the spring **white flowering dogwoods** on the far shores are in bloom.

Finally, the rushing water itself makes for an excellent subject as it flows past the half-submerged rocks. A medium telephoto lens is best used here to isolate these areas.

If you continue along the road on foot (rather than cross the wooden bridge), you will see the stream pass over some large boulders. This area is usually well-shaded, but on sunny days just enough light filters through to compromise the photographic possibilities of the scene. It is definitely worth investigating, however, because of the way it differs from the more open area on the near side of the bridge.

To the right of the bridge are several **pools of water.** Because of the stillness of the water, this is an excellent place to

photograph fallen leaves or possibly even some reflections of the trees and sky.

Crossing the bridge, you no longer follow the stream initially. The road, 1.5 miles long, leads to the trailhead for **Ramsay Cascades,** which is an 8-mile round-trip (and rather strenuous) walk. Along the way you will pass many trees covered with mosses, and even one covered with ferns. Some of the largest **poplars** grow in this part of the park. In fall, the foliage here is quite dramatic, and, in spring, several stands of **crested dwarf iris** can be found just off the roadside.

The waterfall at trail's end is the highest in the park; the water here drops over 75 feet over ledges and outcroppings of rock all along the way. These cascades may be photographed with the surrounding rocks and foliage—including the **white rhododendron**—or more abstract photographs—e.g., close-ups of the water spraying off the many rocks—can be taken with a telephoto lens.

Mountain laurel, Mount LeConte, 80-200mm lens with bellows, 3 seconds at f/16

MOUNT LeCONTE

The primary attractions of Mount LeConte are its hiking trails and the lodge perched at the top. Five trails go to the top, one to satisfy just about every level of challenge. For overnight visitors, pack llamas lighten the load (unlike mules and horses, llamas are accustomed to high altitude and don't destroy the trail from repeated passage). Dinner and breakfast, kerosene lighting and heating, and seclusion round out the rustic experience of the lodge. **Mount LeConte Lodge** is open from March through October. (Reservations, which are required, can be obtained by writing LeConte Lodge, Box 350, Gatlinburg, TN 37738, or by calling 615-436-4473.)

A short distance from the lodge are two scenic areas, Cliff Top and Myrtle Point. **Carolina rhododendron, painted trillium** and **sand myrtle** are abundant at this altitude. **Myrtle Point,** almost a mile from the lodge, is a good place to photograph **sunrise.** Many birdwatchers, searching for **veery, olive-sided flycatchers** and **chickadees,** also favor this site early in the morning.

Cliff Top, only one-fourth mile from the lodge, is ideal for **sunsets,** but the overgrown trees interfere with long views of the valley below.

Two trails to Mount LeConte pass by waterfalls. The **Rainbow Falls Trail** (6.8 miles one-way) passes by some gorgeous stands of **catawba rhodo-dendron,** especially by Rocky Spur. The **Grotto Falls Trail/Trillium Gap Trail** will take you past, and behind, Grotto Falls.

The shortest hike to Mount LeConte (5.2 miles one-way) is by the **Alum Cave Bluffs Trail.** In June, much of the trail is covered with **rosebud orchid, catawba rhododendron, white rhododendron** and **mountain laurel**. The trail crosses Alum Cave Creek several times in the beginning, then follows it closely past the interesting geological formation known as **Arch Rock.** Here, just 2.5 miles from the beginning, the trail passes under a stone arch—a natural tunnel, really—climbs a bit, then opens up into a large bald of mostly **catawba rhododendron** and **mountain laurel.**

ROARING FORK

For the first-time visitor to the Smokies, or even the seasoned veteran, it is hard to beat the beauty and diversity of the Roaring Fork area. Here one can explore the incredible variety of spring wildflowers or just relax alongside of any number of mountain stream cascades. Traces of the homesteads of many of the early settlers can be found here, as well as evidence of the once-common American chestnut tree.

The **Roaring Fork Motor Nature Trail** is a 5.5-mile road that once served as a wagon trail to the old community of Roaring Fork. Today, the trail is easily reached by leaving Gatlinburg at stoplight No. 8 and following the signs for Cherokee Orchard. A self-guiding map, available from the Park Service, will steer you past old cabins, mills, cascading streams and Grotto Falls —the parking lot of which was once a cornfield. Trillium Gap Trail to Mount LeConte, moss-covered rocks, wildflowers and thickets of mountain laurel and catawba rhododendron are all part of this area of the park that many visitors miss.

Although many wildflowers may be seen along the roadside, an enormous variety can be appreciated in the areas of the established pulloffs, beginning with the **Noah "Bud" Ogle homestead.** The groundcover on the hillside across from the parking area is rich with ferns (mostly **marginal shield** and **tapered ferns**) and contains some **pink lady's slipper** that do not seem to bloom reliably every spring. While these are beautiful, the real reward emerges around the Bud Ogle homestead and along the trail to the tub mill.

The short trail to the old cabin is a nice central point from which to locate the wildflowers in this area. This trail crosses a (usually) dry streambed that is overgrown with tall grass and contains **common strawberry** to the right and **wild geranium** to the left. As you cross over these grasses, you will see a small stand of blue **bird-foot violet** where the trail levels off and plenty of **crested dwarf iris, wild blue phlox, false Solomon's seal, chickweed, white violet** and **Canada violet** scattered about.

Following the streambed back around, and then left to the bottom of the hillside beneath the parking area, you will find several **showy orchis.** One grows on the near side of a small stream, the other across the stream and close against the hillside. This area is also covered with **Jacob's ladder** and several **yellow trillium** scattered toward the dry streambed.

At first sight, the most striking flowers by the cabin are the **white flowering dogwood** and the **redbuds** in the distance across the clearing. Don't let these divert your attention from the less-visible ground flowers. Around the cabin (on the side nearest the parking area) are plenty of **foamflowers.** Close to the back of the cabin may be found **Dutchman's breeches, wild blue phlox, Greek valerian** and **cut-leaved toothwort**— which many people miss because of the thick underbrush.

The trail to the tub mill, which begins by Bud Ogle's cabin, is abundant with flowers. Along the way you will see **large-flowered trillium, downy yellow violet, wood sorrel, foamflowers** and **crested dwarf iris.** Even more photogenic flowers will be found near the tub mill itself.

As you approach the tub mill, you may note several **showy orchis.** Two particularly striking specimens appear on the left, just at the edge of the trail; another grows off to the right in the underbrush

Several smaller trails lead off to the right, each heading to a streambank covered with **bluets, foamflowers** and **Canada violets.** Across the stream you will see stands of **crested dwarf iris,** but you must be prepared to ford the stream to appreciate them fully.

One of the richest stands of **large-flowered trillium** may be found in this area in the clearing by the mill and on the hillside to the left of the trail. Mixed in with the trillium in the clearing are some **long-spurred violet, Canada violet** and **Jack-in-the-pulpit. White violets** and **foamflower** grow all over, particularly by the tree stumps and fallen logs near the mill beside the stream. This area also boasts a number of **bishop's caps,** especially by the tree stumps beside the stream.

The winding road from the Bud Ogle homestead to the Ephraim Bales homestead may be rough on your brakes. If you take your time, though, it should prove rewarding. Essentially, the

Mountain brook, Roaring Fork, 80-200mm lens, 8 seconds at f/22

road follows the stream—usually from a higher elevation but at times at stream-level. This permits you to view and to photograph the stream from a variety of angles.

All along, there are small (one- to two-car) pulloffs. Most of these are across the road from the stream. At these spots you can position yourself over the stream and its hundreds of cascades. Many moss-covered rocks jut out, and they are frequently covered with fallen leaves in autumn.

In the spring, the **mountain laurel** and **catawba rhododendron** bloom, providing a colorful backdrop against the dark green foliage. Because most of this area is invariably in deep shade, it is impossible to predict exactly when the blossoms will appear (usually late June/July) or which plants will bloom.

Two popular stops on the **Motor Nature Trail** are Grotto Falls and Rainbow Falls. Grotto Falls is an easy 3-mile round-trip walk through a **hemlock** and **poplar** forest; Rainbow Falls is a slightly more challenging 5.5-mile round-trip walk along LeConte Creek. **Grotto Falls** provides a unique opportunity to walk behind the falls, and the water from **Rainbow Falls** creates a rainbow in afternoon sunlight as it falls 80 feet to LeConte Creek; both are worth seeing.

The **Place of a Thousand Drips** is a colorful name for an area on the left side near the end of the Motor Nature Trail. Water usually seeps from every crack and crevice of this moss- and lichen-covered cliff, making it very photogenic. From a pulloff just past these falls, if you stand with your back to The Place of a Thousand Drips, you will see the water below and understand why this a favored place for photographing the stream in the distance through the trees. A variety of wildflowers grow along the mountainside here, including some **wild ginger** about one-fourth mile above the pulloff.

Toward the end of the Motor Nature Trail stands the **Ephraim Bales homestead.** Now a collection of old wooden buildings, it was once a working farm. From the

Dogwood, Sugarlands, 80-200mm lens, 1 second at f/16

clearing in front of the main cabin, a foot-path angles back to the road. On either side of this path may be found **yellow trillium, Jack-in-the-pulpit** and many nice stands of **large-flowered trillium,** which often turn pink with age. Along the trail, especially near where it meets the road, are several small groupings of **showy orchis.**

Behind the cabin runs a stream with some impressive cascades. The best place to photograph this scene is downstream from the cabin, where several cascades are lined up together. The ideal photographic vantage is the middle of the stream; the stream and cascades are framed by the foliage along the sides and trees at the top.

SUGARLANDS

The park headquarters, visitor center and ranger's offices are in the Sugarlands area, where the road from Gatlinburg to Cherokee meets the road to Cades Cove. This is a place where cameras get packed away before guests visit the restroom facilities, view the short park-orientation film or browse through the gift-shop; the fact remains, however, that it is a prime place for photographing trees.

Sugarlands, named for the abundance of **sugar maple** trees, is in a valley, or cove, surrounded by hardwoods. In the fall, the **poplars** on the mountainsides are transformed into a myriad of colors, and the treelines become very distinct. In the spring, these same mountainsides become a patchwork of green of all possible shades. By positioning yourself in the field in front of the visitor center, you can very easily capture the changing seasons.

Be sure not to overlook the area just in front of the visitor center. In the fall the **sweet gum** trees frequently take on particularly good color. Very striking images can result by photographing them against the dark background of the hillsides in shadow. In the spring, the same approach can be used to photograph the **white flowering dogwoods** which abound.

Cataract Falls is just a short walk behind the ranger's offices, and the trail passes by some beautiful **white rhododendron.** The Sugarlands self-guiding **nature trail** is only 1 mile round trip; beginning behind the visitor center, it crosses Fighting Creek. Both are easy walks and make for a nice introduction to the park if you are short on time.

Long-tailed salamander, Chimneys area, 80-200mm lens with bellows, 2 flash units, 1/60 second at f/11

Mountain ash, Clingmans Dome, 80-200mm lens, 1 second at f/16

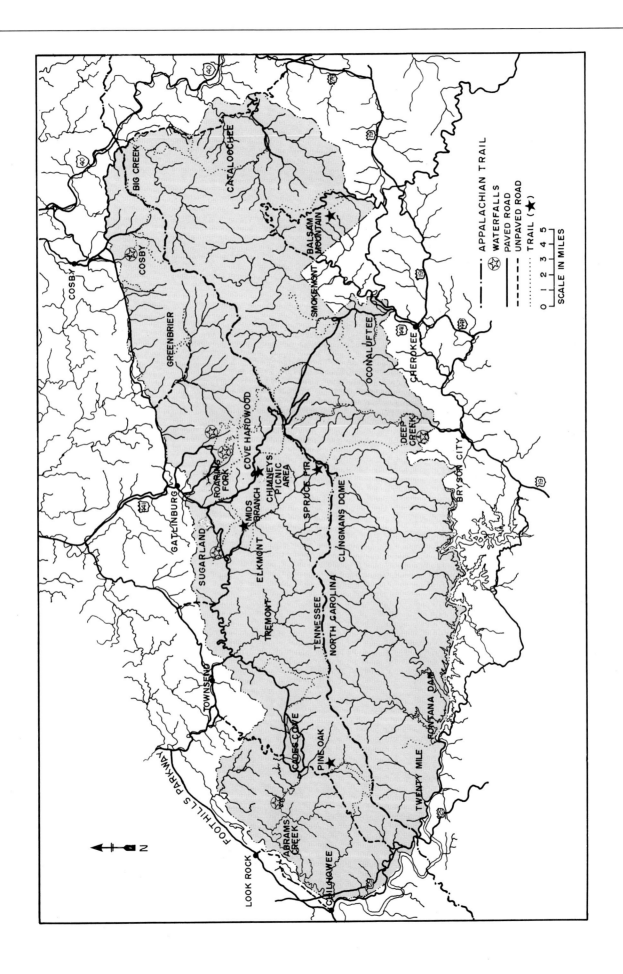

SUGGESTED READINGS

PHOTOGRAPHY

Angel, Heather. (1982). *The Book of Nature Photography*. London: Ebury Press.

Freeman, Michael. (1984). *The Wildlife and Nature Photographer's Field Guide*. Cincinnati, OH: Writer's Digest Books.

Grimm, Tom. (1979). *The Basic Book of Photography*. New York: New American Library, Inc.

Izzi, Guglielmo, & Mezzatesta, Francesco. (1981). *The Complete Manual of Nature Photography*. Translated by Adrian A. Bertoluzzi. New York: Harper and Row.

O'Hara, Pat. (1987). *The Place of Blue Smoke: Great Smoky Mountains National Park*. Text by Tim McNulty. San Rafael, CA: Woodlands Press in association with Great Smoky Mountains Natural History Association.

Shaw, John. (1984). *The Nature Photographer's Complete Guide to Professional Field Techniques*. New York: Amphoto.

Shaw, John. (1987). *John Shaw's Close-ups in Nature*. New York: Amphoto.

NATURAL HISTORY

Albright, Rodney, & Albright, Priscilla. (1984). *Walks in the Great Smokies*. Charlotte, NC: East Woods Press.

Brewer, Carson. (1983). *Hiking in the Great Smokies*. Knoxville, TN: S.B. Newman Printing Co.

DeLaughter, Jerry. (1986). *Mountain Roads and Quiet Places*. Gatlinburg, TN: Great Smoky Mountains Natural History Association.

Huheey, James E., & Stupka, Arthur. (1967). *Amphibians and Reptiles of the Great Smoky Mountains National Park*. Knoxville, TN: University of Tennessee Press.

Murlless, Dick, & Stallings, Constance. (1975). *Hiker's Guide to the Smokies*. San Francisco: Sierra Club Books.

Sharp, Aaron J., Campbell, Carlos C., & Hutson, William F. (1972). *Great Smoky Mountains Wildflowers*. Knoxville, TN: University of Tennessee Press.

Stevenson, George B. (1969). *Ferns of the Great Smoky Mountains National Park*.

Stupka, Arthur. (1963). *Notes on Birds of the Great Smoky Mountains National Park*. Knoxville, TN: University of Tennessee Press.

Stupka, Arthur. (1964). *Trees, Shrubs and Woody Vines of the Great Smoky Mountains National Park*. Knoxville, TN: University of Tennessee Press.

INDEX